Frameworks of the European Union's Policy Process

This book advances the state of the European Union's policy theory by taking stock of seven promising frameworks of the policy process, systematically comparing their limitations and strengths, and offering a strategy to develop robust research agendas. Frameworks may constitute competing policy explanations depending on assumptions they make about EU institutional and issue complexity. The frameworks include detailed analyses of multi-level governance, advocacy coalitions, punctuated equilibrium, multiple streams, policy learning, normative power Europe, and constructivism. Besides generating a fertile dialogue that transcends the narrow confines of EU policy, contributions highlight the value of intellectual pluralism and the need for clear and rigorous explanations of the policy process.

This book was previously published as a special issue of the *Journal of European Public Policy*.

Nikolaos Zahariadis is professor and director of the political science program at the Department of Government, University of Alabama at Birmingham, USA. He is the co-chair of the public policy section of the European Union Studies Association, former president of the International Studies Association-South, a Fulbright scholar, a Policy Studies Organization Fellow, and the recipient of numerous honors and awards for his work on comparative public policy.

D1088820

Journal of European Public Policy Series
Series Editor: Jeremy Richardson is a Professor at Nuffield College, Oxford
University

This series seeks to bring together some of the finest edited works on European Public
Policy. Reprinting from Special Issues of the *Journal of European Public Policy*, the focus
is on using a wide range of social sciences approaches, both qualitative and quantitative, to gain a comprehensive and definitive understanding of Public Policy in Europe.

Frameworks of the European Union's Policy Process

Competition and Complementarity across the Theoretical Divide

Edited by
Nikolaos Zahariadis

Routledge
Taylor & Francis Group

LONDON AND NEW YORK

First published 2014
by Routledge

Published 2014 by Routledge
2 Park Square, Milton Park, Abingdon, Oxfordshire, OX14 4RN

and by Routledge
711 Third Avenue, New York, NY 10017

Routledge is an imprint of the Taylor and Francis Group, an informa business

First issued in paperback 2015

British Library Cataloguing in Publication Data
A catalogue record for this book is available from the British Library

ISBN 978-0-415-71923-0 (hbk)
ISBN 978-1-138-95470-0 (pbk)

Typeset in Garamond
by Taylor & Francis Books

Publisher's Note
The publisher accepts responsibility for any inconsistencies that may have arisen during the conversion of this book from journal articles to book chapters, namely the possible inclusion of journal terminology.

Disclaimer
Every effort has been made to contact copyright holders for their permission to reprint material in this book. The publishers would be grateful to hear from any copyright holder who is not here acknowledged and will undertake to rectify any errors or omissions in future editions of this book.

Contents

Citation Information

The chapters in this book were originally published in the *Journal of European Public Policy*, volume 20, issue 6 (2013). When citing this material, please use the original page numbering for each article, as follows:

Chapter 1
Building better theoretical frameworks of the European Union's policy process
Nikolaos Zahariadis
Journal of European Public Policy, volume 20, issue 6 (2013)
pp. 807–816

Chapter 2
Twenty years of multi-level governance: 'Where Does It Come From? What Is It? Where Is It Going?'
Paul Stephenson
Journal of European Public Policy, volume 20, issue 6 (2013)
pp. 817–837

Chapter 3
Advocacy coalitions: influencing the policy process in the EU
Patrycja Rozbicka
Journal of European Public Policy, volume 20, issue 6 (2013)
pp. 838–853

Chapter 4
Punctuated equilibrium theory and the European Union
Sebastiaan Princen
Journal of European Public Policy, volume 20, issue 6 (2013)
pp. 854–870

Chapter 5
Ambiguity, multiple streams, and EU policy
Robert Ackrill, Adrian Kay and Nikolaos Zahariadis
Journal of European Public Policy, volume 20, issue 6 (2013)
pp. 871–887

Chapter 6

Constructivism and public policy approaches in the EU: from ideas to power games
Sabine Saurugger
Journal of European Public Policy, volume 20, issue 6 (2013)
pp. 888–906

Chapter 7

A normative power Europe framework of transnational policy formation
Vicki Birchfield
Journal of European Public Policy, volume 20, issue 6 (2013)
pp. 907–922

Chapter 8

Learning in the European Union: theoretical lenses and meta-theory
Claudio M. Radaelli and Claire A. Dunlop
Journal of European Public Policy, volume 20, issue 6 (2013)
pp. 923–940

Please direct any queries you may have about the citations to
clsuk.permissions@cengage.com

Building better theoretical frameworks of the European Union's policy process

Nikolaos Zahariadis

ABSTRACT   We aim to build better frameworks of the European Union's policy process by taking stock of promising theoretical lenses, assessing their strengths and limitations, and developing robust research agendas. Frameworks may constitute competing policy explanations depending on assumptions they make about institutional and issue complexity. Points of competition and complementarity are identified, leading to a research agenda that specifies which lenses to use and when.

INTRODUCTION

In the last 20 years or so, analysts have developed increasingly sophisticated simplifications (frameworks or lenses) of the European Union (EU) policy process, seeking explanatory insight and predictive capability. Contributors to the project assess seven promising frameworks of the EU policy process, taking stock of their strengths and limitations. Key assumptions, variables and their underlying logic are clarified and explored. To develop robust research agendas and build better frameworks, a foundation is laid based on differentiations between issue and institutional complexity.

The contributions have considerable value-added for EU studies. First, this is the first systematic analysis of different frameworks of the EU policy process. Second, the contributors speak to each other and to theoretical developments in the broader field of policy studies, generating a fertile dialogue that transcends the narrow confines of EU policy. Third, contributions highlight the value of intellectual pluralism in policy studies. Choice is viewed as a menu of alternative explanations and methodologies with different trade-offs and not as a right or wrong answer to a given problem. Fourth, the proposed research strategy helps scholars think more clearly and rigorously about ways to develop and systematically compare explanations of the policy process.

1

GOOD FRAMEWORKS AND THEORIES

Frameworks structure diagnostic and prescriptive modes of inquiry, helping to systematically organize distinct ways of thinking about public policy. Theories identify particular elements of importance within each framework that are relevant to a class of questions and specify processes and consequences. Frameworks and theories are hierarchically nested (Ostrom 2007). Each lens may contain several theories, and some lenses are more fully developed than others.

Frameworks help make sense of the policy process. Good frameworks make their assumptions explicit, identify important variables, and clarify the causal logic connecting variables to outcomes, helping analysts anticipate problems, limitations, and consequences. Better frameworks use their panoply of tools to pursue the twin goals of explanation and prediction with equal rigor. In practice, one tends to dominate the other. A medical analogy may fruitfully explain the difference between the two. We know the course of illness when one catches a cold. We can specify the cycle of fever following coughing and sneezing, which in turn is followed by physical weakness and aches. We even have remedies to address the problem. But we still deal with symptoms, not causes. Predictive capability is very high, but explanation remains rudimentary. There is a range of chronic illnesses that have been diagnosed and treated with little hope of finding a cure. Explanation aims at causality. It seeks a deeper understanding of why things work in order to isolate causes from symptoms and develop treatments that address causes rather than alleviate symptoms. In social science, human limitations and the lack of experimental control force us to lower expectations regarding causality and prediction (Simon 1983). We strive to develop knowledge that helps us understand public policy and allows us to address, and dare to hope of one day solving, major social problems. But what is the best way of developing such knowledge?

COMPETING OR COMPLEMENTARY FRAMEWORKS?

Zero-sum intellectual pluralism is the norm in policy studies, fuelling rancorous debates about theoretical hegemony, methodological standards, and disciplinary identity. Analysts are typically more interested in maintaining theoretical orthodoxy or methodological purity than uncovering more compelling answers to real-world problems. We part ways with such efforts. Paraphrasing Dryzek and Leonard's (1988: 1258) commentary on disciplinary history in political science, we begin with the observation that (positive-sum) pluralism is the essence rather than an obstacle to progress in policy studies. It helps provide a platform to a conversation between frameworks and invites analysts to cross boundaries to better assess the benefits and limitations of different lenses. We do not aim to build bridges *per se*, just better frameworks.

So far the architecture of policy knowledge has mostly followed a vertical approach where analysis focuses on a single framework explaining a particular case or event. Scholars identify a flaw or limitation in a particular lens and propose empirically verifiable ways to overcome limitations. But they invariably engage in debates within a particular lens. For example, a proponent of principal–agent approaches might identify the conditions under which the European Commission might succeed in 'imposing' its preferences on members of the Council in matters of competition policy. Another proponent of principal–agent approaches might relax one of those conditions to investigate whether they also apply to problems of taxation policy, where the Commission is theorized to hold less sway. These vertical pillars of cumulation have important but limited value because they tell us a lot about a narrow class of problems but not much about policy in general.

Our project closes this gap by taking an explicitly horizontal approach, which involves a menu of alternative lenses. Each framework makes its own assumptions and generates its own empirical evidence about when it is likely to be useful and why. The aim is to help scholars make good analytical choices, addressing new and old problems in historically contingent environments. But not all frameworks are competing explanations of the same event. Some give complementary answers but only in certain areas.

Ever since Allison's (1971) classic study of the Cuban Missile Crisis, it has been apparent that the ability to apply different perspectives has significant merit. First, understanding different theoretical frameworks forces the analyst to clarify his/her own assumptions. Under what conditions is a particular framework applicable? Are the assumptions descriptively realistic? Do they make sense in this particular case? Second, an explicitly comparative approach encourages the development of competing hypotheses and therefore exposes the strengths and weaknesses of various lenses. Every lens identifies particular variables of significance and specifies the logic that connects them. But lenses cannot and do not explain every EU policy in every instant. Empirically identifying the range of cases a particular lens explains relative to others is a useful exercise because it tells us what to expect, and more importantly it indicates where and how to push the limits of each lens to gain more predictive or explanatory power.

The project has two principal aims. First, we take stock of promising theoretical frameworks of the EU policy process, specify their strengths, and assess their limitations. There have been numerous attempts to create systematic ways to study EU policy, especially since the creation of the *Journal of European Public Policy* in the mid-1990s. Despite movement, however, there has not been much movement forward. Frameworks dedicated to explaining EU policy remain for the most part theoretically underdeveloped and empirically incomplete. Our list is not exhaustive, but it contains the more promising frameworks to date: multi-level governance; advocacy coalitions; punctuated equilibrium; multiple streams; policy learning; normative power Europe; and constructivism. Selection was based on the range of assumptions each framework makes, the number of articles and/or books that have used the lens, ability to speak to the broader policy literature, and the potential scholars claim it has in explaining EU policy. We did not include principal–agent approaches largely because there are very good reviews already in print (e.g., Kassim and Menon 2003; Pollack 2007). The list will not satisfy everyone, but it lays the foundations for a more systematic approach to the study EU policy. Judgment is not passed on the value of any lens; that is for the reader to decide based on information derived from the second objective.

Second, we use the information presented to develop robust research agendas. To what extent are frameworks competing or complementary explanations of similar policy choices? Familiarity with lenses and their limitations will help scholars build more accurate 'arrows in their quiver', so to speak, which they can use to address social problems. This is easier said than done.

In one of the first attempts to explain policy choice from a variety of perspectives, Graham Allison argued that lenses can provide both competing and complementary explanations. At one level, each perspective answers the same question. It contains a different logic of explanation and assigns different weight to relevant factors. Assessing the explanatory power of each perspective enables the analyst not only to gain a better grasp of how and why particular EU policy-makers make the decisions they do, but it also sheds light into predicting what kind of decisions other policy makers are likely to make in the future. At another level, however, different lenses answer different questions. As Allison (1971: 251) claims:

> Spectacles magnify one set of factors rather than another and thus not only lead analysts to produce different explanations of problems that appear, in their summary questions, to be the same, but also influence the character of the analyst's puzzle, the evidence he assumes to be relevant, the concepts he uses to examine the evidence, and what he takes to be an explanation.

The point behind competing versus complementary perspectives is far from trivial. Most analysts who systematically assess the explanatory power of different perspectives tend to view perspectives as competing. But analyses are often pitched at different levels (Peterson 2001). We pitch ours at the same level and still find points of competition and complementarity. Carefully specifying assumptions and identifying the conditions under which each perspective yields important insight are crucial steps in understanding the complexity of making policy (Zahariadis 1998).

INSTITUTIONAL AND ISSUE COMPLEXITY

EU policy-making is very messy because it is characterized by heavy doses of complexity. This is not to say that national policy-making is not messy, but rather the complexity of the EU renders policy-making difficult to understand. EU institutions now have to deal with 27 national systems, each with its own traditions, institutions, styles, values, and timetables. Differences need to be addressed and somehow reconciled in order for policy to be made. Given the complexity of EU rules, procedures, and jurisdictional boundaries, what is surprising is not the rightfulness (or not) of EU decisions but the fact that any decisions are made at all.

Frameworks may be categorized according to how they deal with complexity. Each lens paints a slightly different picture of the EU policy process based on assumptions about institutional and issue complexity. Some frameworks, such as constructivism, assume higher issue complexity, while others, such as principal–agent approaches, may posit higher institutional complexity. At one level, therefore, both constructivists and delegation theorists seek to explain Europe's recent financial crisis. At another level, however, constructivists ask whether the crisis exposes rifts in national ways of making policy, while competence delegation scholars focus more closely on compliance and enforcement mechanisms. For constructivists the problem may be an issue of diverse European identities, but for analysts using principal–agent approaches it is fundamentally a problem of flawed institutional design.

Complexity refers to the nature of interaction among distinct units or parts of a system. Interaction takes place horizontally (across EU institutions) and vertically (between EU and national and sub-national actors). Highly complex systems are characterized by free-flowing information across many units with planned or unexpected feedback loops which are not immediately comprehensible (Zahariadis 2003). Complexity has two dimensions: issue and institutional. Issue complexity refers to the amount and nature of informational linkages and may be operationalized as the degree of information overload. How much information is needed for an issue to be properly understood? How many links are made across issues? How much and what type of information do we need to have before we can start tackling a particular problem? As the number of links increases, the number of potential participants to the process also increases. This phenomenon gives rise to two implications. First, decisions are harder to arrive at when the number of participants rises. Agreement is difficult to achieve not simply because more people now need to agree but also because decision-makers will more likely contest the frames of the debate. Second, the direction of policy change becomes more unpredictable as links connect different types of information and point to potentially different solutions. Issue boundaries fluctuate, activating participants with different goals, raising the prospect of political conflict, and increasing the marginal elements of competing coalitions. As issue linkages increase, actor strategies change (McKibben 2010) and temporal valuation of the process is sharpened. Advocates for the EU *status quo* have incentives to elongate the process in hopes of paralysis, shifting attention, or policy fatigue. Issue complexity is obviously a politically contestable concept whose value varies across actors, solutions, and problems.

Institutional complexity refers to a multitude of rules governing close interactions among a high number of structurally differentiated units across different organizational levels. It contains such design features as branching, cycling, asynchrony, multi-directionality, and overlap that provide ample opportunities for frames of success and failure to jump across sub-systemic boundaries. An interesting feature of complexity is the notion of feedback. Negative feedback in a system means that an increase in one variable produces a decrease in another. This kind of feedback tends to perpetuate the *status quo*. As disturbances occur – and they are certain to occur – negative feedback returns the system to equilibrium. Predator–prey relationships are a good example of negative feedback mechanisms. Positive feedback promotes self-reinforcing behavior leading further away from the *status quo*. Not only does it alter the balance of power within institutions but it also entrenches ideas that continue to reproduce policies long after problems have been addressed, discarded, or forgotten. Different institutions, and often different units within institutions, have different capacities and channels to receive and process information signals, leading to variable trajectories of positive or negative feedback (Jones and Baumgartner 2005). Although they are distinct dimensions, issue and institutional complexities also feed off each other.

Complexity has four implications for the study of EU policy. First, increasing complexity raises cost because more actors are involved and in different, potentially contradictory ways. Although expertise and competence affect EU agency autonomy (Wonka and Rittberger 2010), more autonomous agencies naturally place more demands on resources. Moreover, different organizational needs lead to shifts in cost from producing and collecting to tracking and standardizing relevant information. Second, complexity begets complexity. It is politically less contentious to add new or more bureaucratic structures, protocols, rules, or fail-safe systems than it is to remove or reduce existing structures. Reducing or significantly modifying existing structures yields political opposition from disaffected actors. Although it is monetarily costlier, it is politically more expedient to simply add new or more rules onto the existing ones especially if costs are widely distributed through national budgets. Third, higher complexity gives rise to political conflict. More information and unanticipated feedbacks create overlapping and nested institutional jurisdictions that raise the specter of power struggles for control of agendas and resources. Venue-shopping, contested policy frames, and strategic inconsistency complicate, and may hinder, co-operation (Alter and Meunier 2006). Fourth, complexity safeguards diversity. If 'united in diversity' is a key EU aim, citizens and their national leaders have incentives to sustain complex processes in the hope of saving national idiosyncrasies and values from the homogenizing pressures of economies of scale. In other words, complexity of issues and institutions is as much a utilitarian instrument of EU governance as it is a strategic tool of identity construction.

WHICH WAY FORWARD?

Contributions take stock of promising theoretical frameworks of the EU policy process. Each author articulates the unit and level of analysis, specifies assumptions regarding institutional and issue complexity, elaborates on the key concepts and propositions of the lens, elucidates the causal driver that links variables to outcomes, assesses strengths and weaknesses, and charts a course for future research. Most of the frameworks originally aimed to explain national policy-making processes. Are they sufficiently robust to explain the EU process as well? Do they need to be significantly altered to serve as adequate explanations? Or do we need to discard them altogether and develop EU-specific frameworks?

Each framework deals differently with complexity. On a practical level, one way to cope with high levels of complexity is systemic paralysis, which effectively re-nationalizes policy. Such a state of affairs forces issues to be addressed through the principle of subsidiarity; that is, at the lowest possible governmental level. Indeed, some (not only Euroskeptical) member governments have at times deliberately blocked decisions, such as those pertaining to corporate taxation, to retain control of what they consider to be critical issues of national sovereignty. However, it is clear that the locus of decision-making and consequently power have over time shifted toward the EU without examples of rollback (Stone-Sweet 2004: 236). The shift has taken place through treaties, adjudication, bureaucratic 'creep', and political negotiation. But integration is uneven across issues (Majone 2009), having been accomplished largely through accretion, not rational design. The end result has not been a more centralized, democratic, efficient, or effective system of policy-making (Scharpf 1999). Rather a fluid 'garbage can' has emerged, mixing solutions, problems, and participants at different times for different purposes to arrive at decisions (Richardson 2006). The point is not that the Commission gains or national governments lose. Institutions interact in different ways across diverse issues at historically contingent times to produce outcomes that replicate, amend, or reject specific national policies in favor of solutions that express acceptable trade-offs among common EU values. In the absence of legitimate coercion, as is the case with national democracies, the end result is a malleable and perennially contested quest to make policy that rationalizes, co-ordinates, perpetuates, and ritualizes complexity.

Paradoxically, this shift upwards has not been accompanied by the emergence of strong political leadership at the EU level. The reason is subterfuge (Héritier 1999). Many important issues are acrimoniously debated at the EU level. However, while decisions are fiercely fought at the collective level, implementation remains mostly in national hands. Processes of monitoring and compliance are in place, but they are often weakly and unevenly enforced (Falkner *et al.* 2005). In such a policy-making system, leadership plays the subdued role of maintaining the system rather than the more politically active role of brokering solutions. Even the recent financial crisis has produced more fanfare than substance in finding ways to deal with the risk of monetary collapse. As long as the process allows national leaders to achieve European integration and still retain national control, there are no incentives for substantive change.

Looking at this state of affairs, Richardson (2006: 25) claims: 'the complexity of the EU policy process means that we must learn to live with multiple models and learn to utilize concepts from a range of models in order to help us describe it as accurately as possible'. Others prefer a synthetic approach to

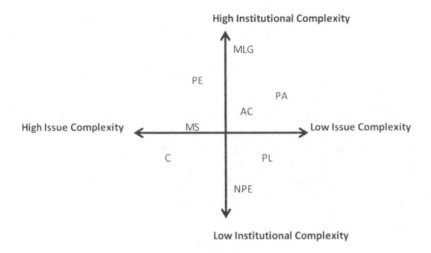

Figure 1 Perspectives and complexity in EU policy

policy (e.g., John 2003). We chart a third way. It specifies which lenses to use and when, based on what the different frameworks say through the filters of institutional and issue complexity.

The strategy begins by identifying areas of similarities and differences among lenses included in this project. Frameworks that share critical assumptions on one or both dimensions may be viewed as competing explanations of the same phenomenon (Figure 1). We also include the principal–agent framework in the Figure owing to its wide use albeit with a question mark because it is not elaborated here. Explanatory or predictive power may be empirically assessed by testing lenses side-by-side in an effort to ascertain which lens explains and predicts more with less. Frameworks with significant differences may be considered complementary because they ask fundamentally different questions. They may not be fruitfully compared because they illuminate different aspects of policy and are applicable under different conditions. For example, Figure 1 shows the multi-level governance and punctuated equilibrium approaches may be viewed as competing on issues involving higher institutional complexity. Constructivism and policy learning are competing explanations in cases of lower institutional complexity. Policy learning and multiple streams are complementary as they diverge on assumptions about institutions and issues.

Our project lays the foundations of the strategy by identifying competing and complementary frameworks. Future research may test and replicate the empirical validity of our claims in order to more carefully delineate the explanatory and predictive capability of each competing lens. This can be done with a nested 'most/least likely' case design. The process resembles the sequencing of what Jupille *et al.* (2003) term two models of dialogue: domain of applicability (to fully specify the range of conditions and expectations); and then competitive testing (to assess explanatory and predictive power). Our contribution lies in proposing complexity as the lynchpin of holding the agenda together. The design involves selecting cases where the lens is expected to fit and then a range of cases where it does not. For example, constructivism and multiple streams may be positioned to explain the highly complex issue of the current financial crisis. They can then be paired to examine employment schemes under cohesion policy, an area of high institutional complexity, and decisions to save endangered species, an area of lower institutional complexity. Results isolate the effects of institutions and highlight limitations regarding issue complexity. The aim is to identify limitations under similar conditions in order to clearly ascertain the trade-offs each lens makes between explanatory and predictive power.

The next step is to improve what each lens lacks by relaxing its assumptions and using different analytical techniques to clarify its logic or confirm its hypotheses. Complementary lenses may be used to more clearly describe different (not necessarily sequential) policy aspects of the same issue and more accurately explain or predict outcomes. Competing lenses can then be rank-ordered, subsumed, or discarded. The reader is invited to pass judgment on each author's argument by constructing his/her own experiments assessing empirically the strengths and weaknesses of each lens and utilizing our strategy. The effort to prove us wrong will not only advance the state of policy theory but also help build better frameworks of the EU policy process.

Biographical note: Nikolaos Zahariadis is professor and director of political science at the Department of Government, University of Alabama at Birmingham, USA.

ACKNOWLEDGMENTS

Special thanks to the Office of the Dean of Arts and Sciences and the Department of Government at UAB and the Center for European and Transatlantic Studies at Georgia Tech for their financial support of a workshop on this topic in Birmingham, Alabama, 9–10 March 2012. Alasdair Young and the workshop participants supplied the perfect feedback, intellectual climate, and collegial patience with my unending requests to make this project possible.

REFERENCES

Allison, G.K. (1971) *Essence of Decision*, Boston, MA: Little, Brown.

Alter, K.J. and Meunier, S. (2006) 'Nested and overlapping regimes in the transatlantic banana dispute', *Journal of European Public Policy* 13(3): 362–82.

Dryzek, J.S. and Leonard, S.T. (1988) 'History and discipline in political science', *American Political Science Review* 82(4): 1245–60.

Falkner, G., Treib, O., Hartlapp, M. and Leiber, S. (2005) *Complying with Europe*, Cambridge: Cambridge University Press.

Héritier, A. (1999) *Policy-making and Diversity in Europe*, Cambridge: Cambridge University Press.

John, P.C. (2003) 'Is there life after policy streams, advocacy coalitions, and punctuations? using evolutionary theory to explain policy change', *Policy Studies Journal* 31(2): 481–98.

Jones, B.D. and Baumgartner, F. (2005) *The Politics of Attention*, Chicago, IL: University of Chicago Press.

Jupille, J., Caporaso, J.A. and Checkel, J.T. (2003) 'Integrating institutions: rationalism, constructivism, and the study of the European Union', *Comparative Political Studies* 36(1/2): 7–40.

Kassim, H. and Menon, A. (2003) 'The principal–agent approach and the study of the EU: promise unfulfilled?', *Journal of European Public Policy* 10(2): 121–39.

Majone, G. (2009) *Integration by Stealth*, Oxford: Oxford University Press.

McKibben, H.E. (2010) 'Issue characteristics, issue linkage, and states' choice of bargaining strategies in the European Union', *Journal of European Public Policy* 17(5): 694–707.

Ostrom, E. (2007) 'Institutional rational choice: an assessment of the institutional analysis and development framework', in P.A. Sabatier (ed.), *Theories of the Policy Process*, Boulder, CO: Westview, pp. 21–64.

Peterson, J. (2001) 'The choice for EU theorists: establishing a common framework for analysis', *European Journal of Political Research* 39: 289–318.

Pollack, M. (2007) 'Principal–agent analysis and international delegation: red herrings, theoretical clarifications, and empirical disputes', *Bruges Political Research Papers No. 2*, Bruges: College of Europe.

Richardson, J. (2006) 'Policy-making in the EU: interests, ideas and garbage cans of primeval soup', in J. Richardson (ed.), *European Union: Power and Policy-making*, London: Routledge, pp. 3–30.

Scharpf, F.W. (1999) *Governing in Europe: Effective and Democratic?*, Oxford: Oxford University Press.

Simon, H.A. (1983) *Reason in Human Affairs*, Stanford, CA: Stanford University Press.

Stone-Sweet, A. (2004) *The Judicial Construction of Europe*, Oxford: Oxford University Press.

Wonka, A. and Rittberger, B. (2010) 'Credibility, complexity, and uncertainty: explaining the institutional independence of 29 EU agencies', *West European Politics* 33(4): 730–52.

Zahariadis, N. (1998) 'Comparing three lenses of policy choice', *Policy Studies Journal* 26(3): 434–48.

Zahariadis, N. (2003) 'Complexity, coupling, and the future of European integration', *Review of Policy Research* 20(2): 285–310.

Twenty years of multi-level governance: 'Where Does It Come From? What Is It? Where Is It Going?'[*]

Paul Stephenson

ABSTRACT   In two decades since the Maastricht Treaty, multi-level governance (MLG) has developed as a conceptual framework for profiling the 'arrangement' of policy-making activity performed within and across politico-administrative institutions located at different territorial levels. This contribution examines the ways in which the MLG literature has been employed, effectively taking stock of applied research to date. It identifies five main uses of MLG and the different focus of emerging research over time. Considering the most recent scholarship, the contribution explores possible new directions for research, in light of global governance, culminating in a 'bird's eye view' of MLG over 20 years.

1.   INTRODUCTION

No other term in the study of European policy-making, perhaps in modern European political studies, has gained common currency like multi-level governance (MLG). As a concept it offers a palatable, easily digestible paradigm for grasping how the European Union (EU) works in practice. And yet, it has not been interpreted and applied in the same way by all scholars. Generally speaking, in face of both the *issue complexity* and *institutional complexity* of policy activity in the EU *vis-à-vis* national policy-making, MLG has been used to try to provide a simplified notion of what is pluralistic and highly dispersed policy-making activity, where multiple actors (individuals and institutions) participate, at various political levels, from the supranational to the sub-national or local. It implies spatial distinctions and geographical separation but, at the same time, its most vital feature is the linkages that connect levels. MLG implies engagement and influence – no level of activity being superior to the other – and, therein, a mutual dependency through the intertwining of policy-making activities.

To permit a sartorial analogy, MLG has been thrown around by scholars like a favourite coat – a staple item in the European political science wardrobe, but perhaps one worn so often that it has now become threadbare. Does it still do the job as it once did – covering the body (providing an explanatory framework), fulfilling the essential task of keeping out the draughts (accounting for the logic of institutional configurations)? This contribution explores the various uses of MLG and how they have changed over time. Given the wealth of academic output on, or relating to, MLG, the contribution discusses how it has been 'taken up' from various academic perspectives and concerns, with illustrative examples. In the latter part, it identifies areas where MLG may have further application for helping to overcome complexity and ambiguity in international policy-making.

Every scholar makes their own literature review, and no two lists are identical. The added value of this analytical review is its examination of how MLG has been embraced by a *wide range* of scholars and used in *different ways* over time, regardless of the original intentions of Gark Marks and Liesbet Hooghe, arguably the king and queen of multi-level governance. The selection of material is based on the novelty and significance of scholarship in terms of how it seeks to tackle institutional or issue complexity in the EU's multi-level system, but also how MLG has been reconciled with other sets of literature.

2. MLG SINCE MAASTRICHT: WHERE DOES IT COME FROM? WHAT IS IT?

In the 20 years since its first mention in an academic article (Marks 1993), the multi-level governance (MLG) literature has mushroomed. Its founders soon recognized competing visions of the concept (Marks and Hooghe 2004). MLG emerged as a vertical arrangement and a way to convey the intimate entanglement between the domestic and international levels of authority. It gave us a simplified way of understanding what European policy-making looked like on a day-to-day basis in (certain) policy areas, were we to slice the EU down the middle to obtain a cross-section of governance activity. Some derided MLG for its lack of predictive powers, asserting that it offered little explanation of causality, and, by consequence, classified it as a *mere* concept rather than a theory. This is arguably unfair because other prevalent frameworks (advocacy coalitions, policy networks, normative power) in policy analysis may have significant explanatory power to account for policy-making processes and actor/issue complexity, but do not necessarily aim at prediction either – even grand theory did not set out explicitly to peer into the future; rather neofunctionalism and intergovernmentalism evolved as lenses for interpreting the past. Thus, even if MLG could not provide a toolkit to help scholars explain the precise dynamics of *how govern-ance arrangements had come to be*, what it could tell us was *how governance was arranged today* in a way that was easy to grasp, i.e., how the EU was perform-ing as a 'polity' and 'machinery' (Kohler-Koch and Eising 1999: xii). In short, it overcame complexity.

The last five years has seen several 'retrospectives' of MLG. Conzelmann and Smith (2008) have taken stock and looked ahead, with a focus on structural funds and environmental policy. Piattoni (2009) has offered a historical and conceptual analysis that identifies the dichotomies of centre/periphery, state/society, domestic/international in multi-level governance, plotting them along three axes. Kohler-Koch and Larat (2009) have explored the diversity of research traditions in Europe and how MLG had been used in national research. Enderlein, Wälti and Zürn's (2010) 31-chapter edited 'handbook' has examined MLG from domestic and EU perspectives, but also regarding comparative regionalism and global governance. Bache and Andreou (2011) have uncovered nascent and emerging patterns of MLG across South-East Europe. Finally, Levi-Faur's (2012) recent 52-chapter volume, to which Bache (2012) also contributed, has examined MLG within the broader notion of *governance*, bringing in considerations of risk, regulation, markets and civil society.

While the 'first generation' of scholarship was caught up with the novelty of new governance forms and how they could transform basic institutional structures – perhaps in a rather introspective way – the 'second generation' of literature steered MLG towards new modes of governance and regulation (Conzelmann 2008: 26–7). To talk of *generations* is useful when attempting to group literature and draw out the main focus and applications. However, given the wealth of MLG literature after 20 years, it is now difficult to pinpoint precisely where one generation ends and another begins, particularly since some scholars may have used MLG for similar purposes over the entire period. Moreover, not all scholars are united in debate and exchange. Given the delays inherent in academic publishing, one should also be wary of fixing cut-off points. Instead, the most one can hope to do is identify when new uses of the literature first occur; any temporal dimension will be a 'loose sequence' of emergent scholarship. This second section examines four main uses of MLG, each with two focal points, while acknowledging the interconnectedness of themes and overlap in the literature.

2.1. Original uses (1993–)

2.1.1. *Legal jurisdictions of authority and efficiency*
Marks and Hooghe's (2004) original conceptualization of multi-level governance steered EU political studies away from the long-running theoretical ping-pong that fixated on proving the convincingness of intergovernmentalism or neofunctionalism to explain integration over 40 years. Three important events had just taken place. First, the reform of the Structural Funds in 1988 placed greater emphasis on partnership and co-ordination, bringing pressure to reform administrations and create rules and procedures for the shared management of structural funds. Second, the creation of the single market with the '1992' programme saw the mobilization and proliferation of interest groups within policy networks. Third, the signing of the Treaty on European Union in February 1992 spawned the concept of 'subsidiarity' or rather, the political desirability of policy action at the lowest possible level.

Against this political backdrop, Mark's 1993 article entitled 'Structural Policy and Multi-Level Governance in the EC', analysed the then recent developments in the EC's 'structural policy', essentially asking two sets of questions: the first, 'How have institutional innovations come about, and which actors have been most responsible for shaping them?'; and the second set of three inter-related questions, 'What are the consequences of institutional innovation for existing institutions? What kind of political order is emerging in Europe? What are the consequences of institutional innovation for the existing state system?' Marks argued for the analysis of institution building to go beyond areas transparently dominated by the member states, i.e., financial decisions, major pieces of legislation and the treaties. Recognizing 'the increasing importance of subnational levels of decision-making and their myriad connections with other levels', he suggested the emergence of *multi-level governance* – 'a system of continuous negotiation among nested governments at several territorial tiers' as a result of 'a broad process of institutional creation and decisional reallocation that had pulled some previously centralized functions of the state' up and down (Marks 1993: 392).

This first article was soon followed by other scholars' explorations of MLG as an alternative to traditional state-centric forms of government (Marks *et al.* 1996), in light of its actor-centred (institutional) dimension (Marks 1996; Sharpf 1997a) and its obvious applicability to EU cohesion policy close-up (Hooghe 1996). MLG offered a conceptual framework (way of seeing) for studying European regional (cohesion) policy (Bache 1998; Benz and Eberlein 1999) and accounting for the broader transformation from 'government' to 'governance' and even 'metagovernance' (Bache and Flinders 2004; Jessop 2004; Kohler-Koch and Eising 1999). Together, Hooghe and Marks's (2001) consolidated volume encouraged a comparative investigation of institutional adaptation between the national and regional level (Börzel 2002), and the supranational and national level (Kohler-Koch 2003). In a nutshell, MLG captured the state's own 'unravelling', i.e., it was no longer tightly centralized and/or performing all functions at the highest level; like a coat whose thread had got caught, its main body being pulled apart.

Hooghe and Marks (2003: 234) recognized the inadequacy of political science responses to what was occurring, with the stretching of 'established concepts over the new phenomena'. Whereas federalists sought to explain developments in power-sharing among and within states, International Relations (IR) scholars extended theories of international regimes to account for the 'diffusion of authority within states'. How to explain that more flexible arrangements were emerging – was it a question of rational choice on the grounds that governance could be more efficient by varying the territorial scale and degree of centralization? The authors distinguished between: *general purpose jurisdictions* with non-intersecting (static) memberships at a limited number of levels (often rather rigid in their terms of institutional architecture); and *task-specific jurisdictions* of intersecting (fluid) membership with unlimited levels and flexible in design. Type 1 was like a 'Russian doll set' with only one relevant jurisdiction/authority at each level, whereas type 2 was a puzzle made up of many functionally specific pieces, each providing services or solving problems. The first reflected the simplistic nature of state control and the exertion of authority in a unitary state, while the second expressed the layered system of co-existing levels of authority – a complex pattern of transnational, public and private institutional relations with overlapping competences (Hooghe and Marks 2003: 235–6).

2.1.2. *Europeanization and regionalization*

There is an overlap with MLG and the literature on regionalization and Europeanization, particularly since MLG was originally studied with a view to the functional pressures to regionalize in order to accommodate policy, i.e., to create mechanisms enabling the access to, and active participation of regional interests in, the policy process. Three solutions to 'the dilemma of exclusion and inclusion' for multi-level actors were: hierarchical sequencing, flexible association/disassociation and loose coupling. As Benz and Eberlein (1999: 329) assert, empirical studies of subnational political action helped advance MLG, following the build-up of the (then) European Community's regional level engagement in the policy process. MLG emphasized power-sharing and the dispersion rather than accumulation of authority, while Europeanization brought new patterns of inter-organizational linkages and saw the dynamics of mutual adjustments (patterns of adaptation) made by institutions as a result of multi-level interactions (Jordan 2001). The challenges for domestic structures to secure political representation and co-ordination included overcoming horizontal divisions and conflicts between/within regional politico-administrative bodies, and repairing distant and/or distrustful vertical relations between national and supranational levels.

It is no coincidence that much of the literature emerging at this time from regional studies scholars (Keating and Loughlin 1997) and on interest representation (Greenwood 2003) tied into MLG debates, at a time when hundreds of regions were establishing a physical presence in Brussels through their own offices. This phenomenon challenged established state-centric assumptions of international relations, sparking greater interest in 'intermediate level innovation', while MLG 'assumed the meaning of a conceptual umbrella'. The 'impressive extension' of the multi-level governance framework allowed it to be used to interpret and explain Europeanization processes, with the result that scholars 'devoted' greater attention 'to the diverse, contradictory and anything but linear trajectories of institutional change and institutionalization' (Gualini 2003: 418). With more complex and varied electoral arenas, political parties needed new strategies to perform effectively in 'multi-layered systems'; however, MLG was 'very much a party-free zone' (Deschouwer 2003: 213; see also Hepburn 2008). In short, MLG was about opportunities for some and loss (of power and influence) for others, leading to potential conflict, blocking and, subsequently, strategies to circumvent the national level whereby lower levels sought to increase their institutional and negotiating capacity.

Building on earlier work, where he termed the phrase 'flexible gatekeeping', Bache (1998) reconciled MLG with Europeanization in a study of cohesion policy in the United Kingdom (UK) and the EU. He noted the rise in flexible type 2 arrangements ('loose neocorporatism') across local governance in the 1990s with the 'revival' of English regions. However, one could not assume causality between MLG pressures from Brussels and the process of devolution, which had long been part of the UK's domestic political agenda (Bache 2008: 156). The author criticized MLG for failing to distinguish between *governance* and *participation* (or dialogue); what was missing from the debate were empirical indicators. If governance implied *engagement*, how could one measure the exertion of influence, and gauge the outcomes of participation in decision-making processes when power relations were ill-defined and with so little insight into the links between actors? Bache (2008: 162) saw policy networks as an obvious bridge between MLG and Europeanization. Warleigh-Lack (2008) later advocated combining MLG with policy networks, the complexity and plurality of networks in MLG implying a 'push and pull' between institutions.

2.2. Functional uses (1997–)

2.2.1. *Policy/country studies and implementation studies*
From the outset, MLG was used extensively to analyse institutional arrangements for the implementation of structural funds in cohesion policy, uncovering diverging formal and informal rules at the national and supranational level to explain multi-level tensions. So successful was MLG that it soon entered into the language of policy-makers. The Committee of the Regions today organizes annual 'ateliers' to bring together scholars and practitioners to celebrate – and in so doing legitimize – multi-level governance. It considers MLG to mean co-ordinated action by the supranational institutions with national, regional and local authorities, based on partnership and aimed at drawing up and implementing EU policies (Warleigh 1999). The focus on co-ordination and partnership at various stages of the policy-making process, including (re-)formulation and implementation, implies pluralistic interactions, different institutional levels coming together to 'govern', be it in a functional and administrative capacity.

Through several rounds of enlargement, academic analyses of MLG shifted from the old to new member states in Eastern and South-East Europe. Yet, country case studies showed the persistence of central control in the face of diverging subnational practices. Regionalization processes triggered *differentiation*, resulting in very varied administrative governmental capacities across multiple arenas (Benz and Eberlein 1999; Milio 2010; Piattoni 2008; Stubbs 2005; Taylor *et al.* 2012; Thielemann 1999). MLG was applied extensively in environmental policy (Fairbrass and Jordan 2004; Knill and Tosun 2008), but also in other 'first pillar areas' such as telecoms policy (Fuchs 1994), food safety (Bernauer and Caduff 2004) and innovation policy/leadership (Kaiser and Prange 2004). Attempts were even made to apply it to international relations (Welch and Kennedy-Pipe 2004), economic policy (Perraton and

Wells 2004), demand and supply (Rosenau 2004), international trade policy (Knodt 2004), common foreign security policy (Smith 2004) and climate change governance (Kern and Bulkely 2009). In short, there is a clear overlap here with the original focus on regionalization, or, rather, the administrative process and consequences of implementing EU policy.

2.2.2. *Problem-solving, co-ordination, learning*

In MLG's relative infancy, Scharpf (1997b) explored its problem-solving capacity, arguing that its effectiveness at different governance levels varied from one policy area to the other. He identified constraints on both national and European capacity in a range of policy domains, offering a two-dimensional conceptualization of multi-level problem-solving capacities – a move away from bargaining towards positive-sum games. Scholars observed a shift from national policy control to European level co-ordination – in transport, telecoms and energy infrastructures. Exploring the impacts of non-regulatory policies at the member state level, Conzelmann (1998) examined the changing context of regional policy, noting how multi-level consensus on policy solutions reduced conflict.

Scholars examined learning in the context of MLG (Paraskevopoulos 2001). Schout (2009) focused on variations across governance level, policy instrument and organization type, questioning how instruments were designed and used in the EU's multi-level system. Had the so-called 'governance turn' delivered on its promises of enabling better problem-solving? To answer these questions, one needed to consider the sociological aspects of MLG – structures, processes and procedures – as well as leadership. Egan (2009: 1248) noted how, because of the growth of transnational networks, policy learning was taking place in multiple venues; co-operation and interaction was fostering the exchange of ideas, technical expertise and information, as well as the promotion of norms and values. He referred to cross-national networks of collaboration at the international level that were emulating, copying, borrowing and imitating their neighbours. Indeed, MLG encouraged experimentation, to overcome political and financial 'stalemates' through exposure to ideas from outside that could transform the understanding of self-interest (Zito and Schout 2009: 1115). With MLG now reconciled with 'networked governance' (Jordan and Schout 2006), policy-making was considered a *process* involving self-organizing, multi-level actors – and one which signalled a move away from 'hierarchical steering' towards communication-based instruments.

2.3. Combined uses (2001–)

2.3.1. *New modes of governance*

One might argue that the open method of co-ordination (OMC) introduced at Lisbon in 2000 was MLG's first serious contender as a rival governance framework. This new approach saw the EU as 'heterarchical' and 'decentred', with OMC 'radicalizing' the process of subisidarity (Hodson and Maher 2001: 719).

'Soft' policy instruments not backed by EU legislation encouraged co-ordination, benchmarking and best practice without any threat of sanctions. Yet, Kaiser and Prange (2004) found the multi-level governance character of innovation policies a major stumbling block to applying OMC – in fact vertical policy co-ordination *and* horizontal policy learning could not occur. MLG enabled non-hierarchical linkages for interdependent policy co-ordination, but it appeared scholars had underestimated the conditions needed to ensure effective policy co-ordination and, hence, convergence, such were the massive variations among member states and regions in terms of budgetary powers and legal competencies. The authors identified vertical co-ordination problems including increasing transaction costs, which rose with 'the number of administrative levels and degree of subnational autonomy' (*ibid.*: 250).

Beyond social and employment policy, which were trialling OMC, private organizations as well as public bodies were becoming important actors. Multi-level actors were competing heavily for critical resources (knowledge, research, finance, entrepreneurs, etc.), but there was a mismatch or 'tension' between political ambitions and market reality. It was uncertain if one could achieve critical mass with such dispersed authority. How would long-established innovation policies at the level of the German *Länder* react to top–down policies cooked up in Brussels? (*ibid.*: 255–7).

OMC had promoted transparency via data exchange, benchmarking and best practice both vertically between governance layers, and horizontally across 27 member states. One could thus conceive of the EU as a 'multi-level information environment' in which communication and data processing were determined by dimensions of complexity (density, structurability, heterogeneity), as explored by Blom *et al.* (2008). MLG empowered subnational actors by bringing them into decision-making arenas, and giving them greater access to information, i.e., knowledge: 'informal and disorderly governance *relates to and overlays* orderly and formal governance' (Bache 2008: 163). Héritier and Rhodes (2011) have asked how and where informal governance sits in MLG's tightly coupled institutional construct 'in the shadow of hierarchy'. Defining governance as a specific mode of production of norms and public goods created via co-production, where the co-producers transcend different levels, the authors recognized the growing importance of public–private decision networks involving many types of public authority.

2.3.2. *New institutionalism/principal–agent theory*

In Schmitter's (2004) scheme of regional integration 'multi-level and polycentric governance' sits at the centre of a box containing six types of institutionalism (rational, historical, epistemic, legal, political and sociological). MLG is here defined as:

> an arrangement for making binding decisions which engages a multiplicity of politically independent but otherwise interdependent actors – private and public – are at different levels of territorial aggregation in more-or-less

continuous negotiation/deliberation/implementation, and that does not assign exclusive policy *compétence* or assert a stable hierarchy of political authority to any of these levels. (Schmitter and Kim 2005: 5)

Schmitter stressed the spatial (polycentric nature of the EU), pluralistic (no single collective institution) and functional dimensions (delegated tasks). MLG's popularity was supposedly owing to its descriptive neutrality and thus, 'putative compatibility with virtually any of the institutional theories and even several of their more extreme predecessors', i.e., its strength was its malleability and impartiality, while its limitation was its explanatory power and insight. For politicians, Schmitter and Kim (2005: 5) conceded, it also avoids the controversial word 'state' and 'sounds a lot less forbidding and threatening'.

Blom-Hansen (2005: 644) used principal–agent theory (found in rational choice institutionalism) to break MLG's 'virtual monopoly' on analysing cohesion policy. He conceded that while this MLG 'paints a descriptively accurate picture of the cohesion policy's complex implementation structure, it fails to specify which actors, at which levels, will be causally important'. A principal–agent framework helped focus on control mechanisms and potential implementation deficits (*ibid.*: 625). Moreover, MLG was criticized for equating multi-level *involvement* (in decision-making) with multi-level *governance*, and failing to specify *why* certain levels are empowered and others weakened. Acknowledging that 'cohesion policy involves a chain of principal–agent relationships, ranging from the European Council to local authorities', he advocated more studies to reveal domestic institutional relationships, rather than focusing on the supranational level. More specifically, how did rules and resources influence control, and determine the dynamics of MLG? (*ibid*: 629–30).

Acknowledging MLG as a 'reconfiguration of policy-making space in the EU', and perceiving of institutions as 'honey pot sites', Awesti (2007: 1) proposed a framework for understanding MLG from three institutional perspectives, to 'test' MLG. First, he asserted that from the conceptual lens of *rational choice institutionalism (RCI)*, polycentric governance emerges out of explicit choices made by national leaders in view of perceived functional benefits, and noted how Marks (1996: 28) himself had hypothesized that authority may be reallocated if it is seen to have 'politically salient pareto beneficial consequences' such as 'reduc[ing] transaction costs or increas[ing] the efficiency of policy provision' (Awesti 2007: 11–12). Second, path dependency is present in MLG since institutional structures and processes become difficult to modify. From an *historical institutionalist perspective* (Pierson 1996), MLG arrangements get 'locked-in' as a permanent feature of the EU policy system, as actors adapt socially to procedures and norms, while the cost of exit gradually increases; governance arrangement becomes 'sticky' (Awesti 2007: 13–17). In cohesion policy, the norm of 'generalized reciprocity' based on exchange and mutual expectations, persists over time, transforming zero-sum relations

(Paraskevopoulos 2001: 260). Third, from a *sociological institutionalist perspective*, actor behaviour in MLG is practised, experienced and replicated: subnational actors in turn exert pressure that favours the further dispersal of authority away from the centre; MLG becomes self-reinforcing as actors, such as policy officers and decision-makers, learn to function according to the behavioural rules of MLG, which encourages highly dense and frequent interaction. Arguably, MLG has itself become a normative feature or value of the EU (Awesti 2007: 17–19). That said, legalistic traditions, deeply entrenched institutional rules and norms at different levels can still obstruct new domestic–supranational relations (Thielemann 1999: 402).

2.4. Normative uses (2003–)

2.4.1. *Legitimacy, democracy, accountability*

The *White Paper on European Governance* (Commission 2001) contained recommendations to enhance democracy and increase the legitimacy of the institutions in the wake of the dissolution of the Santer Commission. Soon after, Olsson (2003) examined 'paradoxes' of MLG in the system of EU structural funds implementation, from a democracy perspective, to see how the burgeoning literature on democracy renewal could be reconciled with MLG. The issue was 'often unproblematized' – if democracy was discussed, it was regarding the basic character of the EU (or perhaps applied to the European Parliament), rather than power and policy-making processes (Olsson 2003: 284). The author saw MLG as essentially top–down and technocratic, but with democratic institutions marginalized; 'democratizing' MLG would mean regulating partnerships or challenging the partnership principle introduced in 1998 with the parliamentary principle, to give policy implementation more democratic legitimacy.

Peters and Pierre (2004) saw MLG as compromising democracy and called it a 'Faustian bargain' – had policy-making sold its soul? Harlow and Rawlings (2006) recognized an 'accountability deficit' in MLG which had itself become organized around self-organizing, self-regulating networks. With governance essentially about co-operation and co-ordination, traditional government control systems were 'undermined'. In fact, not more than 17 per cent of the 1,600 projects in the Connex database on EU governance addressed democracy (Kohler-Koch 2006). Papadopoulos (2008) criticized the scholarly focus in MLG research on managerial concerns of performance and efficiency. Increasing networks in MLG meant governance was 'uncoupled' from the democratic circuit owing to its weak visibility, poor presence of citizen representatives and prevalence of 'peer review' (which relates to the earlier discussion of OMC). MLG 'inhibited' accountability, which required democratic (political) control as well as administrative, fiscal and legal control (Papadopoulos 2008: 40); the fragmentation of power resources between levels meant technocrats were not really politically accountable.

Heinelt (2008) argued that political science reflections should not concern the achievement (or not) of policy objectives – which may be sufficient for applied policy studies or efficiency-oriented analyses of inputs and outputs – but rather 'the basic political logic of governing public affairs in the multi-layered spheres of EU politics' (Heinelt 2008: 54). Acknowledging the *institutional complexity* of MLG, and the 'context-related choices faced by groups of actors so that they can influence purposefully and act interactively', he advocated research to address actor-related capabilities by examining the social environment, available policy instruments and existing institutional settings; one needed to examine MLG endogenously to see what politically determined opportunities and constraints in policy-making, including the 'varying desires, knowledge and perceptions of the multitude of involved actors' who distribute the various tasks and competences between different nested levels (Heinelt 2008: 54–6).

2.4.2. *Identity politics (community, collective identities, political parties, public sphere)*

Finally, it is perhaps fitting that the last of the eight focal points on MLG literature brings us back to Hooghe and Marks (2008), who, in recent work, have explored the possibility of a 'postfunctionalist theory of European integration' – acknowledging an inclement political climate where things have gone 'from permissive consensus to constraining dissensus'. They refer – as they did at the outset – to the articulation of authority across 'jurisdictions' or the 'jurisdictional architecture', and take up the 'building blocks' of multi-level governance, while seeking to reduce complexity and direct attention to one particularly important causally-powerful factor: *identity*. The duo asserts that, while governance concerns the efficient delivery of collective benefits, it is also an *expression of community*. Give its functional rationale, MLG should better acknowledge how the optimal *human co-ordination of resources and tasks* does not necessarily coincide with the territorial scope of community – 'doing' European integration means mobilizing identity, particularly where existing regional political structures of authority are inappropriate, be it inefficient or unconvincing/conflicting. The authors explicitly acknowledge citizens and identity in their definition of governance as 'binding decision making in the public sphere' (Hooghe and Marks 2008: 2), while recognizing that the political experience of MLG – and the research it generated – dismantled many of the original assumptions: first, that public attitudes were superficial and irrelevant; second, that integration was an issue of low salience for the public; and third, that issues emerging from integration were unrelated to basic political conflict between parties, institutions and regions. In short, the EU is system of MLG 'driven by *identity politics* as well as functional and distributional pressures' given that 'community and self-governance, expressed in public opinion and mobilized by political parties, lie at the heart of jurisdictional design' (Hooghe and Marks 2008: 23).

2.5. MLG so far: summing up

The legal and economic ideas providing the rationale for multi-level governance meant that the academic literature was taken up widely in public administration and policy analysis. Political science theories have since been brought in tandem with MLG, to see how they might inform each other, while a more critical literature has been preoccupied with certain social and political philosophical concerns over MLG.

Thus, MLG captured, and simplified, the spatial configurations of policy-making activity, not just decision-making. This implied the dispersal and redistribution of powers and competences to different levels of policy-making activity, and roles for both existing and newly-created institutions and bodies, i.e., of interconnected public and private actors. Acknowledging the emergence of policy communities and issue networks in the EU, calls were made for MLG to be reconciled with the literature on policy networks (Warleigh-Lack 2008). Conceptually, networks were supposed to be non-hierarchical, but in reality, only some enjoyed agenda-setting and decision-making powers; others were *merely* active in implementation. The complexity and plurality of networks in MLG implied a certain 'push and pull' between institutions; but while MLG was lauded as promoting participation, and sustaining the momentum for ongoing co-operation and consensus, it invariably led to conflict and resistance. Indeed, MLG destabilized, fragmented and restructured existing organizational patterns, challenging the existing concentration of power/authority with the opportunities and threats it represents. It also altered political culture and organizational behaviour, bringing new values to policy-making.

From a normative point of view, MLG has burgeoned on the premise of functional efficiency, accountability and democratic legitimacy. Indeed, the functional requirements of implementing many policies have demanded massive politico-administrative reorganization at lower levels, and hence the Europeanization – and to a degree harmonization – of spaces and their units of control. MLG has led to varying degrees of centralization and decentralization. Newly organized territorial structures have bolstered MLG, but in some cases changes in domestic structures cannot always be explained by the EU but by internal pressures for change – as such we must not discount the role of identity in *enabling* MLG. While MLG has been used widely for the analysis of policy-making in former first pillar areas that are institutionally complex, it cannot wholly account for – and is not particularly representative of – policy-making activity in more complex (high politics) issue areas, such as foreign policy or trade and development, where subnational levels have fewer competences.

Finally, while MLG emerged in the literature to account for transformation in the distribution of authority on grounds of efficiency, and with a functional *logic* (as would support argument within rational choice institutionalism), subsequent literature adopted a more sociological focus, examining organizational and social learning, and identity/community, making bridges with both the public policy literature in the field that was evolving in parallel in the 1990s, as well as the earlier seminal work on functionalism/neofunctionalism – indeed, after 15 years, the focus on learning takes us almost full circle to the role of élites in institutionalism, their desires and norms.

3. CURRENT AND FUTURE MLG SCHOLARSHIP: WHERE IS IT GOING?

MLG began by analysing arrangements for implementing the structural funds. Today most major recipients are flailing in the wake of the global financial and euro crises. This has brought home how the EU's fate is intrinsically linked to international politics and economics. MLG no longer operates in splendid isolation as a three-layered, Eurocentric, isolated vision of policy-making, but acknowledges external actors in global governance (GG). The most recent scholarship, in the last five years, has examined transformations from a comparative perspective at the *macro* and *micro level*. This section thus introduces a fifth use of the literature around two additional focal points.

3.1. Comparative uses (2007–)

3.1.1. *Global governance and international institutions*
MLG is being used in the context of globalization and development, international law, finance and trade, exploring its relevance and application outside Europe. Almost a decade ago, Knodt (2004) sought to 'emancipate' MLG from its structural policy origins, to better consider the international context. Analysing the World Trade Organization, she examined how the EU's international embeddedness influenced its own institutional change and the formal organization of European decision-making. Recently scholars have adopted a more concerted international outlook (Enderlein 2010). This seems logical when so many policy issues are transnational, and require solutions from the international community through global governance mechanisms. Kaul (2010: 323) has provided *lessons for* MLG by analysing the changing role of the United Nations (UN) as it struggles to adapt to a new world order where states act 'as intermediaries between national interests and global policy demands'. Slaughter and Hale (2010: 358–9; emphasis added) recognize that what distinguishes MLG's functional, autonomous units from '*mere* issue networks' is 'a certain durability of the arrangement and process' – while transgovernmental networks in the EU may be vertical, 'the real world' (i.e., international policy-making today) is characterized by both vertical and horizontal arrangements in what the authors call, a 'governance matrix'. Beisheim, Campe and Schäferhoff (2010: 370) have revisited transnational public–private partnerships (PPPs), and consider them a type 2 form of MLG governance, 'whereby non-state actors co-govern along with state actors for the provision of collective goods and adopt governance functions that have formerly been the sole authority of sovereign states'. Such PPPs are found in global alliances and project partnerships initiated by the UN Development Programme and World Bank for water management and planning. The authors explore

PPPs' 'virtues and deficits', identifying conditions under which they can be effective and legitimate MLG instruments.

Economic policy-making, not traditionally a first pillar policy, is now 'almost by definition' an area of multi-level governance, according to Enderlein (2010: 423–4). Offering three examples – fiscal federalism (subnational and national level), Economic and Monetary Union in Europe (regional level) and international monetary co-operation and global economic governance (supranational) – he asks 'if economic policy-making *could* and *should* be considered as a single MLG system, or whether one can really treat them as analytically separate' (emphasis added). Arguably, we can't. Spendzharova (2011), in her examination of the multi-level dimension of the European financial crisis, discusses international financial institutions in the same breath as domestic financial sectors, alongside euroscepticism and civil society at the subnational level. She pinpoints the tension between greater centralization of authority at higher levels of governance versus regulatory autonomy at lower levels.

So is multi-level governance now the same as global governance (GG)? Is there simply now a fourth or fifth politico-administrative or technocratic level? Zürn (2012) thinks not. For GG to be multi-level, two conditions must be met: first, the global level must possess authority of its own, beyond mere intergovernmental co-ordination, and with a delegation of powers; second, there should be interplay within the system that demonstrates a division of labour across the levels. Nonetheless, GG can be prescribed as a specific form of MLG when global institutions possess and exert political authority.

3.1.2. *EU & regionalism*

Scholars have been using MLG to make comparative analyses of other regions, using the EU as the yardstick. De Prado (2007: 215) had conceived of global MLG when comparing trends in the EU with those in Asia, but argued that a gradual transformation towards a new world order should be theorized by a 'knowledge-based global multi-level governance paradigm', recognizing that a 'knowledge revolution catalysed by information and communications technologies' will give rise to more transnational actors and regional processes, all influencing governance at various inter-related levels. For Sbragia (2010: 268), the concept of MLG is 'especially tricky' when examined outside of the EU. The dynamics of MLG are very different in the North American Free Trade Agreement (NAFTA), given the 'ironclad commitment to avoid institutionalization and institution-building'. Mercosur is not even a free trade area though highly 'inter-presidential', dependent on personal intervention. Its largest states – Brazil and Argentina – are highly decentralized, a *de facto* limitation to any extensive arrangement of governance functions vertically. As for the 'developing world', scholarly research is too underdeveloped to make any serious evaluation of MLG (Sbragia 2010: 269); the most obvious comparison is the Associations of Southeast Asian Nations (ASEAN), which bears few institutional similarities to the EU, relying heavily on norm diffusion and developing consensus to promote change and integration (Schreurs 2010). Meanwhile,

Obydenkova (2010) claims regionalism in post-Soviet Eurasia represents a form of MLG because it includes different institutional layers (supranational and trans-subnational) and groups of actors (governmental and non-governmental). Where vertical integration has failed, horizontal integration has been successful: the Commonwealth of Independent States is unique in that sovereignty and independence among states has *not* been the starting point, nor has economic integration. Can MLG help explain why there has been little progress in over two decades, despite the 'undeniable advantages of integration' *(ibid.*: 293)?

3.1.3. *Looking ahead: administrative processes, tasks and interactions*
Finally, MLG scholarship long hovered above multi-level institutions, treating each institutional actor as a unitary body. Further scholarship might examine actors *inside* institutions to see how individual and collective identities are asserted, forged and transformed through functional processes of problem-solving and task distribution. Indeed, focussing on the earlier stages of policy-making rather than implementation would suggest an approximation with the agenda-setting literature on images and venues (Baumgartner and Jones 1993). Scholars have called for more attention to be paid to mapping administrative interactions *throughout the policy process*, and identifying what practical types of decision-making are involved. Littoz-Monnet (2010), in her exploration of the notion of 'dynamic multi-level governance', proposes a model called 'reversed intergovernmentalism' that would better account for how actions between venues at multiple levels – including the inter-national – actually lead to decisions, rather than analysing what happens next (*ibid.*: 4).

Heidbreder (2011) acknowledges the *persistent* differences between 27 increasingly interdependent national systems. She calls for a more comprehensive understanding of the EU as a 'multi-level public administration', to better distinguish policy-making procedures; her typology of 'supranational instrumentation' differentiates between explicit versus implicit supranational rule (*ibid.*: 710). One might bring in role theory (Biddle 1986) to reinforce actor-centred analyses of multi-level public administrations, such as recently applied in EU foreign policy (Juncos and Pomorska 2010). Since MLG implies a variety of tasks depending on the configuration of actors at particular points in policy-making time and space, we might consider more practically oriented, interactions-based perspectives of MLG that shed light on the specifics of task-based activities, to illustrate more comprehensively the *when, where* and *what* of governance. Heinelt and Lang's (2011) empirical study already improves our understanding of MLG in practice by comparing regional actor constellations across *different phases* of EU cohesion policy. Focusing on operational programmes, the authors account for variations in governance arrangements in cohesion, non-cohesion and Central and Eastern European (CEE) countries. In short, further research might dig deeper still into the functional aspects of 'doing policy', adopting more sociological considerations and acknowledging ontological questions, including the different ways actors

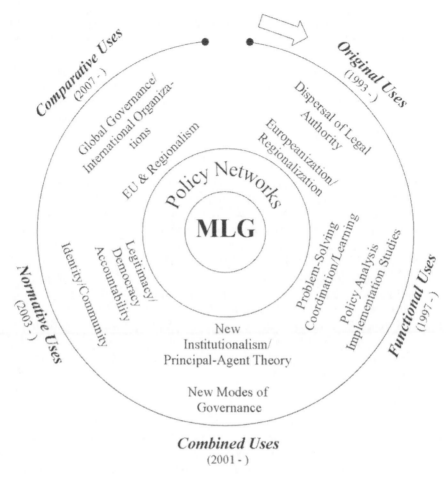

Figure 1 A bird's eye view of MLG's uses over two decades

engaged in multi-level interactions actually see the EU and their place within it, as well as examining close-up institutional actors' tasks across policy domains throughout the stages of the policy cycle.

Figure 1 offers a visual representation of MLG scholarship, in which the five 'uses' and 10 'focal points' have been loosely sequenced, distinguishing between original, functional, combined, normative and comparative uses of the MLG literature. The bird's eye view of multi-level governance captures the evolution in scholarship over time.

4. CONCLUSION

The landscape of European governance has been transformed in two decades. The original concept of MLG has been used by scholars in diverse ways.

The increasing issue and institutional complexity of EU policy-making activity can no longer be captured through an isolated, three-layered conceptualization. Scholars are beginning to analyse the interdependence of the EU with global institutions and governance. There is a need to hone in, through more applied research, to the incremental and pluralistic nature of MLG, to consider the degree to which issue complexity may determine or shape institutional arrangements. This may mean appropriating the existing literature with international relations, or else with sociology and public administration, in order to better grasp institutional/actor complexity. MLG as a conceptual garment of European political science may need 'accessorizing', or to be worn inside out, to provide a new look – one that maintains its relevance and usefulness for this season's policy analysis, wherever the EU is going.

Biographical note: Paul Stephenson is Assistant Professor at the Department of Political Science, Maastricht University.

ACKNOWLEDGEMENTS

I wish to thank Nikolaos Zahariadis and the anonymous reviewers for their helpful comments on early drafts. I am particularly grateful to Tod Hartman for his help turning my original pencil sketch into Figure 1.

NOTE

*After 'Where Do We Come From? What Are We? Where Are We Going?', Paul Gauguin's most famous painting; the expression of a highly individualistic mythology and the culmination of his thoughts (1897/8).

REFERENCES

Awesti, A. (2007) 'The European Union, New institutionalism and types of multi-level governance', *Political Perspectives* EPRU 2(8): 1–23.

Bache, I. (1998) *Politics of European Union Regional Policy: Multi-level Governance or Flexible Gatekeeping?* Sheffield: Continuum.

Bache, I. (2008) *Europeanization and Multilevel Governance: Cohesion Policy in the European Union and Britain*, Lanham, MD: Rowman and Littlefield.

Bache, I. (2012) 'Multi-level governance in the European Union', in D. Levi-Faur (ed.), *Oxford Handbook of Governance*, Oxford: Oxford University Press, pp. 628–41.

Bache, I. and Andreou, G. (eds) (2011) *Cohesion Policy and Multi-level Governance in South East Europe*, Oxford: Routledge.

Bache, I. and Flinders, M. (eds) (2004) *Multi-level Governance*, Oxford: Oxford University Press.

Baumgartner, F. and Jones, B. (1993) *Agendas and Instability in American Politics*, Chicago, IL: University of Chicago Press.

Beisheim, M., Campe, S. and Schäferhoff, M. (2010) 'Global governance through public–private partnerships', in H. Enderlein, S. Wälti and M. Zürn (eds), *Handbook on Multi-level Governance*, Cheltenham: Edward Elgar, pp. 370–82.

Benz, A. and Eberlein, B. (1999) 'The Europeanization of regional policies: patterns of multi-level governance', *Journal of European Public Policy* 6(2): 329–48.

Bernauer, D. and Caduff, C. (2004) 'European food safety: multi-level governance, re-nationalization or centralization?' *CIS Working Paper*, available at http://www.cis.ethz.ch/publications/publications/WP3_Bernauer_Caduff.pdf (accessed 20 October 2011).

Biddle, B. (1986) 'Recent developments in role theory', *Annual Review of Sociology* 12: 67–92.

Blom-Hansen, J. (2005) 'Principals, agents, and the implementation of EU cohesion policy', *Journal of European Public Policy* 12(4): 624–48.

Blom, T., Radulova, E. and Arnold, C. (2008) 'Theorizing modes of governance in the EU: institutional design and informational complexity', *European Governance Papers/Eurogov, 1-34*.

Börzel, T. (2002) *States and Regions in the European Union: Institutional Adaptation in Germany and Spain*, Oxford: Oxford University Press.

Commission of the European Communities (2001) 'European governance. A white paper' *COM(2001)428*, Brussels: European Commission.

Conzelmann, T. (1998) 'Europeanisation' of regional development policies? Linking the multi-level governance approach with theories of policy learning and policy change', *EIoP* 2(4), available at http://eiop.or.at/eiop/texte/1998-004a.htm (accessed 10 October 2011).

Conzelmann, T. (2008) 'A new mode of governing? Multi-level governance between cooperation and conflict', in T. Conzelmann and R. Smith (eds), *Multi-level Governance in the European Union: Taking Stock and Looking Ahead*, Baden Baden: Nomos, pp. 11–30.

Conzelmann, T. and Smith, R. (eds) (2008) *Multi-level Governance in the European Union: Taking Stock and Looking Ahead*, Baden Baden: Nomos.

De Prado, C. (2007) *Global Multi-level Governance: European and East Asian Leadership*, Tokyo: United Nations University Press.

Deschouwer, K. (2003) 'Political parties in multi-layered systems', *European Urban and Regional Studies* 10(3): 213–26.

Egan, M. (2009) 'Governance and learning in the post-Maastricht era?', *Journal of European Public Policy* 16(8): 1244–53.

Enderlein, H. (2010) 'Economic policy-making and multi-level governance', in H. Enderlein, S. Wälti and M. Zürn (eds), Handbook on *Multi-level Governance*, Cheltenham: Edward Elgar, pp. 423–40.

Enderlein, H., Wälti, S. and Zürn, M. (2010) *Handbook on Multi-level Governance*, Cheltenham: Edward Elgar.

Fairbrass, J. and Jordan, A. (2004) 'Multi-level governance and environmental policy', in I. Bache and M. Flinders (eds), *Multi-level Governance*, Oxford: Oxford University Press, pp. 147–64.

Fuchs, G. (1994) 'Policy-making in a system of multi-level governance – the Commission of the European Community and the restructuring of the telecommunications sector', *Journal of European Public Policy* 1(2): 177–94.

Greenwood, J. (2003) *Interest Representation in the European Union*, Basingstoke: Palgrave Macmillan.

Gualini, E. (2003) 'Challenges to multi-level governance: contradictions and conflicts in the Europeanization of Italian regional policy', *Journal of European Public Policy* 10(4): 616–36.

Harlow, C. and Rawlings, R. (2006) 'Promoting accountability in multi-level governance: a network approach', *European Governance Papers*, available at http://www.connex-network.org/eurogov/pdf/egp-connex-C-06-02.pdf (accessed 20 April 2012).

Heidbreder, E. (2011) 'Structuring the European administrative space: policy instruments of multi-level administration', *Journal of European Public Policy* 18(5): 636–53.

Heinelt, H. (2008) 'How to achieve governability in multi-level policymaking: lessons from the EU structural funds and EU environmental policy', in T. Conzelmann and R. Smith (eds), *Multi-level Governance in the European Union: Taking Stock and Looking Ahead*, Baden Baden: Nomos, pp. 53–69.

Heinelt, H. and Lang, A. (2011) 'Regional actor constellations in EU cohesion policy: differentiation along the policy cycle', *Central European Journal of Public Policy* 5(2): 4–29.

Hepburn, E. (2008) 'The rise and fall of a "European of the Regions"', *Regional and Federal Studies* 18(5): 537–55.

Héritier, A. and Rhodes, M. (2011) *New Modes of Governance in Europe: Governing in the Shadow of Hierarchy*, Basingstoke: Palgrave Macmillan.

Hodson, D. and Maher, I. (2001) 'The open method as a new mode of governance: the case of soft economic policy coordination', *Journal of Common Market Studies* 39(4): 719–46.

Hooghe, L. (ed.) (1996) *Cohesion Policy and European Integration: Building Multi-level Governance*, Oxford: Clarendon Press.

Hooghe, L. and Marks, G. (2001) *Multi-level Governance and European Integration*, Lanham, MD: Rowman and Littlefield.

Hooghe, L. and Marks, G. (2003) 'Unraveling the central state, but how? Types of multi-level governance', *American Political Science Review* 97(2): 233–43.

Hooghe, L. and Marks, G. (2008) 'A postfunctionalist theory of European integration: from permissive consensus to constraining dissensus', *British Journal of Political Science* 39: 1–23.

Jessop, B. (2004) 'Multi-level governance and multi-level metagovernance', in I. Bache and M. Flinders (eds), *Multi-level Governance*, Oxford: Oxford University Press, pp. 49–74.

Jordan, A. (2001) 'The European Union: an evolving system of multi-level governance ... or government?' *Policy and Politics* 29(2): 193–208.

Jordan, A. and Schout, A. (2006) *The Coordination of the European Union: Exploring the Capacities of Networked Governance*, Oxford: Oxford University Press.

Juncos, A. and Pomorska, K. (2010) 'Secretariat, facilitator or policy entrepreneur? Role perceptions of officials of the Council Secretariat', *EIoP*, 14, Special Issue 1, available at http://eiop.or.at/eiop/index.php/eiop/article/view/2010_007a (accessed 10 February 2012).

Kaiser, R. and Prange, H. (2004) 'Managing diversity in a system of multi-level governance: the open method of co-ordination in innovation policy', *Journal of European Public Policy* 11(2): 249–66.

Kaul, I. (2010) 'The changing role of the United Nations: lessons for multi-level governance', in H. Enderlein, S. Wälti and M. Zürn (eds), *Handbook on Multi-level Governance*, Cheltenham: Edward Elgar, pp. 323–42.

Keating, M. and Loughlin, J. (1997) *The Political Economy of Regionalism*, London: Frank Cass.

Kern, K. and Bulkely, H. (2009) 'Cities, Europeanization and multi-level governance: governing climate change through transnational municipal networks', *Journal of Common Market Studies* 47(3): 309–332.

Knill, C. and Tosun, J. (2008) 'Emerging patterns of multi-level governance in EU Environmental Policy', in T. Conzelmann and R. Smith (eds), *Multi-level Governance in the European Union: Taking Stock and Looking Ahead*, Baden Baden: Nomos, pp. 145–62.

Knodt, M. (2004) 'International embeddedness of European multi-level governance', *Journal of European Public Policy* 11(4): 701–19.

Kohler-Koch, B. (ed.) (2003) *Linking EU and National Governance*, Oxford: Oxford University Press.

Kohler-Koch, B. (2006) 'Research on EU governance: insight from a stock-taking exercise', *Connex Newsletter* 3: 4–6.

Kohler-Koch, B. and Eising, R. (eds) (1999) *The Transformation of Governance in the European Union*, London: Routledge.

Kohler-Koch, B. and Larat, F. (eds) (2009) *European Multi-level Governance: Contrasting Images in National Research*, Cheltenham: Edward Elgar.

Levi-Faur, D. (ed.) (2012) *Oxford Handbook of Governance*, Oxford: Oxford University Press.

Littoz-Monnet, A. (2010) 'Dynamic multi-level governance – bringing the study of multi-level interactions into the theorising of European integration', *EIoP* 14(1), available at http://eiop.or.at/eiop/index.php/eiop/article/view/2010_001a (accessed 15 February 2012).

Marks, G. (1993) 'Structural policy and multi-level governance in the EC', in A. Cafruny and G. Rosenthal (eds), *The State of the European Community: The Maastricht Debate and Beyond*, Boulder, CO: Lynne Rienner, pp. 391–411.

Marks, G. (1996) 'An actor-centred approach to multi-level governance', *Regional and Federal Studies* 6(2): 20–38.

Marks, G. and Hooghe, L. (2004) 'Contrasting visions of multi-level governance', in I. Bache and M. Flinders (eds), *Multi-level Governance*, Oxford: Oxford University Press, pp. 15–30.

Marks, G., Hooghe, L. and Blank, K. (1996) 'European integration from the 1980s: state-centric v. multi-level governance', *Journal of Common Market Studies* 34(3): 341–78.

Milio, S. (2010) *From Policy to Implementation in the European Union: The Challenge of a Multi-level Governance System*, London: Tauris Academic.

Obydenkova, A. (2010) 'Multi-level governance in post-Soviet Eurasia: problems and promises', in H. Enderlein, S. Wälti and M. Zürn (eds), *Handbook on Multi-level Governance*, Cheltenham: Edward Elgar, pp. 292–307.

Olsson, J. (2003) 'Democracy paradoxes in multi-level governance: theorizing on structural fund system research', *Journal of European Public Policy* 10(2): 283–300.

Papadopoulos, Y. (2008) 'Problems of democratic accountability in network and multi-level governance', in T. Conzelmann and R. Smith (eds), *Multi-level Governance in the European Union: Taking Stock and Looking Ahead*, Baden Baden: Nomos, pp. 31–52.

Papadopoulos, Y. (2010) 'Accountability and multi-level governance: more accountability, less democracy?', *West European Politics* 33(5): 1030–49.

Paraskevopoulos, C. (2001) 'Social capital, learning and EU regional policy networks: evidence from Greece', *Government and Opposition* 36(2): 251–77.

Perraton, J. and Wells, P. (2004) 'Multi-level governance and economic policy', in I. Bache and M. Flinders (eds), *Multi-level Governance*, Oxford: Oxford University Press, pp. 179–94.

Peters, B. and Pierre, J. (2004) 'Multi-level governance and democracy: a Faustian bargain?' in I. Bache and M. Flinders (eds), *Multi-level Governance*, Oxford: Oxford University Press, pp. 75–89.

Piattoni, S. (2008) 'The development of the structural funds: a success story?', in T. Conzelmann and R. Smith (eds), *Multi-level Governance in the European Union: Taking Stock and Looking Ahead*, Baden Baden: Nomos, pp. 73–93.

Piattoni, S. (2009) 'Multi-level governance: a historical and conceptual analysis', *Journal of European Public Policy* 31(2): 163–80.

Pierson, P. (1996) 'The path to European integration – a historical institutional analysis', *Comparative Political Studies* 29(2): 123–62.

Rosenau, J. (2004) 'Contrasting visions of multi-level governance', in I. Bache and M. Flinders (eds), *Multi-level Governance*, Oxford: Oxford University Press, pp. 31–48.

Sbragia, A. (2010) 'Multi-level governance and comparative regionalism', in H. Enderlein, S. Wälti and M. Zürn (eds), *Handbook on Multi-level Governance*, Cheltenham: Edward Elgar, p. 267-278.

Scharpf, F. (1997a) *Games Real Actors Play: Actor-Centred Institutionalism in Policy Research*, Boulder, CO: Westview Press.

Scharpf, F. (1997b) 'Introduction: the problem-solving capacity of multi-level governance', *Journal of European Public Policy* 4(4): 520–38.

Schout, A. (2009) 'Organizational learning in the EU's multi-level governance system', *Journal of European Public Policy* 16(8): 1124–44.

Schmitter, P. (2004) 'Neo-neofunctionalism', in A. Wiener and T. Diez (eds), *European Integration Theory*, Oxford: Oxford University Press, pp. 45–74.

Schmitter, P. and Kim, S. (2005) 'The experience of European integration and the potential for Northeast Asian integration', *East-West Center Working Papers* 10: 1–23, available at http://www.eastwestcenter.org/sites/default/files/private/PSwp010.pdf (accessed 10 September 2011).

Schreurs, M. (2010) 'Multi-level governance the ASEAN way', in H. Enderlein, S. Wälti and M. Zürn (eds), *Handbook on Multi-level Governance*, Cheltenham: Edward Elgar, pp. 308–20.

Slaughter, A.-M. and Hale, T. (2010) 'Transgovernmental networks and multi-level governance', in H. Enderlein, S. Wälti and M. Zürn (eds), *Handbook on Multi-level Governance*, Cheltenham: Edward Elgar, pp. 358–69.

Smith, M. (2004) 'Toward a theory of EU foreign policy-making: multilevel governance, domestic politics, and national adaptation to Europe's common foreign and security policy', *Journal of European Public Policy* 11(4): 740–58.

Spendzharova, A. (2011) 'Is more "Brussels" the solution? New European Union member states' preferences about the European financial architecture', *Journal of Common Market Studies* 50(2): 315–34.

Stubbs, P. (2005) 'Stretching concepts too far? Multi-level governance policy transfer and the politics of scale in South East Europe', *Southeast European Politics* 6(2): 66–87.

Taylor, A., Geddes, A. and Lees, C. (2012) *The European Union and South East Europe – The Dynamics of Europeanization and Multilevel Governance*, London: Routledge.

Thielemann, E. (1999) 'Institutional limits of a "Europe with the Regions": EC state-aid control meets German federalism', *Journal of European Public Policy* 6(3): 399–418.

Warleigh, A. (1999) *The Committee of the Regions: Institutionalising Multi-level Governance?* London: Kogan Page.

Warleigh-Lack, A. (2008) 'The EU, ASEAN and APEC in comparative perspective', in P. Murray (ed.), *Europe and Asia: Regions in Flux*, Basingstoke: Palgrave Macmillan, pp. 23–41.

Welch, S. and Kennedy-Pipe, C. (2004) 'Multi-level governance and International Relations', in I. Bache and M. Flinders (eds), *Multi-level Governance*, Oxford: Oxford University Press, pp. 127–144.

Zito, A. and Schout, A. (2009) 'Learning theory reconsidered: EU integration theories and learning', *Journal of European Public Policy* 16(8): 1103–23.

Zürn, M. (2012) 'Global governance as multi-level governance', in D. Levi-Faur (ed.), *Oxford Handbook of Governance*, Oxford: Oxford University Press, pp. 730–74.

Advocacy coalitions: influencing the policy process in the EU

Patrycja Rozbicka

ABSTRACT   The aim of this contribution is to critically evaluate one of the theoretical approaches used to study the European Union (EU) political system and interest groups activity: the advocacy coalition framework (ACF). ACF considers that the outcome of legislative procedures is influenced by the alignment and role played by advocacy coalitions. This contribution assesses the impact of ACF on our understanding of the influences on the EU policy processes, highlighting the strengths and weaknesses of the approach. The main argument is that the ACF, although very useful in studying the EU political system, shows shortcomings when applied to the study of EU interest groups' performance. The contribution ends with a consideration of future directions for theoretical and empirical ACF research, alone and as part of wider integrated theoretical approaches to understanding the dynamics of influence in the EU.

INTRODUCTION: THE PLACE FOR THE ADVOCACY COALITION FRAMEWORK IN EU STUDIES

In the continuously growing field of European Union (EU) policy studies, one of the most promising theoretical approaches is the advocacy coalition framework (ACF). First developed by Sabatier and Jenkins-Smith during the late 1980s and 1990s (Sabatier 1988, 1998; Sabatier and Jenkins-Smith 1993), the ACF is designed to deal with complex intergovernmental and multi-level subsystems involving large numbers of actors and to understand policy changes over a period of a decade or more within a particular substantive domain/subsystem (example: air pollution control, dangerous chemicals regulation). It has been based on the assumption that political actors have relatively complex belief systems. Owing to their beliefs, actors can be aggregated into a number of *advocacy coalitions*, which alignment and roles played in policy processes influence the outcome of legislation.

Is the ACF a helpful framework? Can it contribute to the understanding of the EU policy processes? And more specifically, is it able to explain the EU interest groups influence? The aim of this contribution is to answer those questions and to critically evaluate the advocacy coalition framework as a theoretical approach to the study of EU policy-making. When assessing the contribution of the ACF, the contribution highlights the strengths and weaknesses of the approach in applying it to the participation of interest groups in the EU political system. Until now, two characteristic patterns have emerged from the application of the ACF to EU interest groups studies. On the one hand, scholars provide evidence of the existence of long-term coalitions, which agrees with the ACF's assumptions. On the other hand, more sceptical researchers point towards more *ad hoc*, tentative relations between interest groups and between interest groups and other stakeholders. As a consequence, the argument can be made that the ACF only partially grasps the complexity of those relations.

This contribution begins with an examination of the advocacy coalition framework. The original texts on the ACF authored by Sabatier and Jenkins-Smith are examined and a condensed explanation of the framework is provided. Looking at the framework's premises and goals, the focus is on those elements which might be useful to analyse EU policy-making and EU interest group activity. In the next section of the contribution, the framework is contrasted with the findings of empirical studies on EU lobbying. The ACF has a series of positive elements which allow us to better grasp interest group activities within the EU system. But, it also has a number of shortcomings. Finally, some theoretical approaches are pointed to that complement the weaknesses of the ACF. In closing, the future directions for theoretical and empirical ACF research are suggested, alone and as part of wider integrated theoretical approaches to understanding the dynamics of influence in the EU.

ADVOCACY COALITIONS: THE ORGINAL CONCEPT

The initial version of the ACF emerged as a search for an alternative to the experience-based research that was dominant in policy studies in 1980s. The authors wished to synthetize the best features of the 'top–down' and 'bottom–up' approaches to policy implementation analyses and to attribute to technical information a more prominent role in theories of the policy process (Sabatier 1998: 98). The goal of the framework was to provide a coherent understanding of the major factors and processes affecting policy processes, including problem definition, policy formulation, implementation and revision in a specific policy domain.

Originally, the framework had four basic assumptions (Sabatier 1993: 16; Weible *et al.* 2008: 1). First, understanding the process of policy change requires a temporal perspective of a decade or more. A period of a year or two is too short to clearly visualize links between actors and their mutual interdependence owing to limited resources. Second, the most useful way to think about such long-term policy change is through a focus on *policy subsystems* (the interaction of actors from different institutions who follow and seek to influence governmental decisions in a policy area). The actors within a policy subsystem are grouped into a number of *advocacy coalitions* that consist of individuals who share a particular belief system – i.e., a set of basic values, causal assumptions, and problem perceptions – and who show a non-trivial degree of co-ordinated activity over time (Sabatier 1988: 139). Third, these subsystems include an intergovernmental dimension, meaning they involve all levels of government. Last, public policies can be conceptualized in the same manner as belief systems; that is, as sets of value priorities and causal assumptions about how to realize them (Fenger and Klok 2001: 157–8). Advocacy coalitions attempt to realize those shared policy beliefs by influencing the behaviour of multiple governmental institutions over time (Sabatier 1993: 25; Sabatier and Jenkins-Smith 1993: 212).

There are two prominent elements of the framework: who are the actors in advocacy coalitions; and what beliefs are exactly of concern? Sabatier argues that most coalitions include group leaders, agency officials and legislators from multiple levels of government, applied researchers and journalists. A number of different levels and types of actors is possible as long as they share a set of basic beliefs and engage in joint actions to alter the rules of governmental institutions over time (Sabatier 1993: 25). Thinking in general categories, there are three types of coalition members: *core members, players,* and *tag-alongs* (Hula 1999). *Core members* seek to influence a bill or a key element of legislation. *Players* are satisfied if they can alter a paragraph or two in a bill. *Tag-alongs* seek a 'photo opportunity' to pursue their own narrow goals (Ainsworth 2001). In addition, at any given point in time, a policy subsystem will usually contain a number of individuals and organizations unassociated with any coalition, but the ACF assumes that most will be unimportant over the long term because they will either leave or be incorporated into one of the coalitions (Sabatier 1998: 103).

While the main ACF postulation is that actors are instrumentally rational, the framework draws also on work in cognitive and social psychology. In particular, the ACF assumes that actors' goals are usually complex and that an individual's ability to perceive the world and to process that information is affected by cognitive biases and constraints (Sabatier 1998: 108). Here, the approach builds on the notion of *bounded rationality*. The actors' ability to process and analyse information is limited by time and computational constraints (which often causes simplified heuristics [Weible *et al.* 2009: 122]). Lastly, the ACF assumes that, on salient topics, actors' perceptions are strongly filtered by their pre-existing normative and other beliefs.

The belief systems of various coalitions are organized into a hierarchical, tripartite structure, with broader levels generally constraining more specific beliefs (Sabatier 1998: 103; Sabatier and Jenkins-Smith 1993: 221). At the broadest level, the *deep core* of the shared belief system includes fundamental normative beliefs, such as left/right scale, which operate across virtually all policy domains. Those beliefs are the most resistant to change. At the middle level there are *policy core* beliefs which refer to a coalition's basic normative commitments, causal perceptions and preferred institutional arrangements across a policy domain or subsystems. Because they are fairly general in scope yet very salient, they prove to be much more useful in coalition analysis than the two other beliefs systems (Weible *et al.* 2008: 2). Actors in different coalitions perceive the world through different *lenses* and thus often interpret a given piece of evidence in different ways. As a result, the *policy core* beliefs provide the 'principal glue' of coalitions (Sabatier and Zafonte 1997). At the lowest level, the *secondary aspects* of a coalition's belief system comprise a large set of opinions concerning the seriousness of the problem or the relative importance of various causal factors, policy preferences regarding desirable regulations of budgetary allocations, the design of specific institutions, and the evaluations of various actors' performances.

The stability of *policy core* beliefs is a major element guaranteeing the stability of the programmes or the policy developments supported by the coalition. The policy core attributes of such programmes and policies will not change as long as the dominant coalition which instituted that policy remains in power. In the original version of the framework, the only way to change the policy core was through some shock originating outside the subsystem (Sabatier 1998: 105). However, Sabatier concluded in later studies that the external disturbances are a necessary but not sufficient cause of a change (Sabatier 1998). The external disturbances translate into policy change only when one coalition is capable and willing to exploit them entrepreneurially (Weible *et al.* 2009: 124). When it happens, a change materializes through the replacement of one dominant coalition by another (Radaelli 1999: 666), or the competing coalitions find a compromise that is superior to the *status quo* by devising a positive-sum solution rather than engage in a zero-sum fight (Sabatier 1998).

Some studies present an argument that *policy narratives* could be a causal variable in the policy change. Policy narratives are understood here as the stories that actors put in the picture to make sense of policy issues and underpin policy solutions (Roe 1994). Shanahan *et al.* argue that actors (in political system) use words, images, and symbols to strategically 'craft' policy narratives that resonate with the public, relevant stakeholders and governmental decision-makers, with the aim of 'producing a winning coalition' (Shanahan *et al.* 2011: 536). The narratives are used and reformulated by different stakeholders to present the coalition's position in such a way as to receive the largest possible support, presenting the coalition's solution as more appealing than its alternatives. There is a high degree of correlation between the change of coalitions' status (for example, losing → winning coalition) and policy change. However, the causal impact of such narratives on policy changes has to be yet further explored.

Another characteristic of the ACF is *policy-oriented learning*. It can be defined as a relatively durable alteration of thought or behavioural intention that results from experience and/or new information introduced to the system with regard to the realization or revision of policy objectives (Mintrom and Vergari 1996: 421; Weible 2006: 101). Policy-oriented learning can take place in relation to a variety of factors. The list of possible factors includes testing and refining one's belief system, responding to challenges to one's beliefs (Sabatier 1988: 150–1); experimenting with different policy mechanisms, understanding their performance and, finally, adapting one's belief system on the basis of that understanding (Schlager 1995: 245). Policy-oriented learning is supposed to be larger inside the coalition, where actors are more willing and open towards information and knowledge exchange, than between coalitions. Opposing coalitions have different belief systems; thus, their perceptions of the situation and their preferred solutions are diverse and rarely compatible. Knowledge acquired through policy-oriented learning may be used to press for policy change. However, according to Sabatier (1998), it again requires a willing and capable coalition. Moreover, the change will be minor; it will influence only *secondary aspects* (Weible *et al.* 2008: 3), which have the possibility of modifying *policy core* beliefs, but it is not guaranteed.

According to the ACF, policy subsystems can be divided between *nascent* subsystems – those in process of forming – and *mature* ones – those that existed for a decade or more (Sabatier 1998: 111–14). In order to mature, the subsystem needs to consist of actors who regard themselves as a semi-autonomous community, who share a domain of expertise and seek to influence public policy within the domain over a long period of time. By definition, it has to include specialized sub-units within agencies at all relevant levels of government and interest groups, or specialized sub-units within interest groups, which regard this as major policy topic. Based on these characteristics, Sabatier argued that coalitions cannot simply evaporate (Sabatier 1993). Coalitions can re-evaluate their belief systems, owing to external shocks, and adversarial coalitions may change the leading position, but a coalition's stability over a decade or more is a crucial element of the framework and policy stability. The hypothesis of coalitions' stability refers only to *mature* policy subsystems (Radaelli 1999: 676). Emerging (*nascent*) coalitions that had no time to consolidate can change.

The ACF has several weaknesses. First, the ACF considers policy change as the result of learning processes within and between advocacy coalitions. However, in explaining policy change, the ACF focuses almost exclusively on the structure, content, stability and evolution of the policy belief systems of advocacy coalitions. There is no attempt to explain how actors with similar beliefs overcome collective action problems, co-operate to pursue common strategies and common goals, and how they maintain coalitions (Fenger and Klok 2001: 157; Schlager 1995: 246). The ACF provides a useful guide to the context in which policy change occurs. It highlights how belief structures arise and adjust over time, how they bring stability to policy subsystems. Although the ACF identifies exogenous shocks (a shock originating outside the subsystem) and policy learning as potential sources of policy change, it falls short of explaining under what conditions policy change will actually take place (Mintrom and Vergari 1996: 422). Not all exogenous shocks and not all instances of policy learning translate into policy change. Moreover, the ACF does not help in explaining changes in the composition of advocacy coalitions themselves.

Second, using the ACF to study a particular empirical case is not without costs and limitations. A thorough ACF study includes a complete collection of data through surveys and interviews, which is somewhat costly in terms of available resources. As Weible suggests, given the limited resources, the costs of the ACF analysis can be reduced with 'an abbreviated analysis by gathering qualitative data with just a few dozen interviews and by analysing available documents' (Weible 2006: 114). However, the loss of systematically collected data in an abbreviated analysis will be felt when trying to identify the different policy core beliefs, resources and venues, greatly reducing the utility of the approach.

APPLYING THE ACF TO THE EU POLITICAL SYSTEM

The EU political system can be characterized as having a fluid and open-ended nature, with a broad range of actors who operate at different levels (Cram 2001: 65). It is not solely determined by formal institutional actors, such as the European Commission, the European Parliament or the Council (Hosli *et al.* 2004: 42). There are complex networks of public and private actors and overlapping and interactive sectoral activities which take place between different levels and actors (Marks 1993; Marks *et al.* 1996). Characterizing the interactions between legislators and lobbyists in the EU context is difficult because of the lack of clear institutional structures that guide or constrain behaviour (Ainsworth 2001: 475).

Looking more closely at the EU, one can identify both a vertical and a horizontal dimension. The majority of scholars agree that both dimensions are of importance (Eising and Kohler-Koch 1999). Of the greatest relevance for the ACF is the horizontal dimension, in which public and private actors have a shared responsibility for resource allocation and conflict resolution (Schmitter 2002: 55). The resource allocation and conflict resolution is often based on *deliberation* and *persuasion* put side-by-side with bargaining and realization of interests. It is a model of policy-making in which actors are open to changing their beliefs and their preferences as long as it meets their ultimate goals, and in which good arguments can matter as much as, or more than, bargaining power (see also Pollack 2005: 36).

The multi-level character of the EU political system and its horizontal dimension have become increasingly difficult to assess analytically and empirically. Most frameworks that are employed to study EU politics, like multi-level governance (Hooghe and Marks 2001; Marks *et al.* 1996), variants of institutionalism (Tsebelis and Garrett 2001) or intergovernmentalist theory (Moravcsik 1998), advance our understanding of the EU. But as *theoretical lenses,* they focus on specific factors and aspects of the European Union and address only a limited set of questions about EU policy-making. The ACF gives additional insights, which can complement the other theoretical models and approaches. Virtually all studies dealing with the ACF's application to the EU have been published during the past decade (Füg 2009: 4). This is reason to believe that there is a growing interest in the advocacy coalition framework to study policy-making in 'Brussels'.

Introducing the arguments, the ACF applies well to the complex set of the relationships in the EU. Those relationships are characterized by a large number of actors from multiple levels of government. In the EU, there is clear evidence of coalitions composed of administrative agency officials, interest groups leaders and researchers from various countries forming, for example, environmental or industry based coalitions (Coen 1997; Dudley and Richardson 1999; Peterson 1995). For example, Daviter writes about the biotechnology agenda in the EU and the diversified spectrum of actors involved, including not only 'usual suspects' like environmental non-governmental organizations (NGOs) but also administrations of member states and some sectors of industry (Daviter 2009). Knodt *et al.*, while applying a comparative perspective and seeking for established general patterns of interactions that take place at the EU level, elaborated on the interaction among territorial and functional interest representation in the EU and the co-operation among regional and functional interests (Knodt *et al.* 2011). In the EU, coalitions seek to maximize their advantage by 'venue-shopping' as is depicted in the ACF (Weible 2006). EU research provides evidence that venue-shopping takes place among levels of government and among the different EU institutions (Dudley and Richardson 1996; Mazey 1998).

Second, the ACF puts the largest attention on salient policy problems, those creating conflict between advocacy coalitions. Frequently, these are characterized by substantial complexity and the involvement of large number of actors. These are the types of situations with which resource dependency and institutional rational choice frameworks have difficulty because of the large number of actors and the uncertainties of preference formation. The relevance of policy problems is an important topic for the study of the EU. The importance attached to policy problems affects the bargaining behaviour of different actors participating in the system, as well as the attention the problem receives (Daviter 2007).

The value of the ACF in analysing the complex political system of the EU lies not only in its applicability to policy processes that involve a large number of actors and great uncertainties, but also in the categories it provides when focusing on policy change and types of policy subsystems. The ACF distinguishes between major versus relatively minor policy changes. Nedergraad, in the study of the EU Common Agricultural Policy (CAP), proved that in the EU semi-federal system a high degree of consensus is required to change the policy core (Nedergraad 2008: 179). Similarly, as in the ACF, his conclusion was that advocacy coalitions resist information that challenges the policy core beliefs of decision actors.

The ACF can also shed light on the range of policy initiatives at different levels and in different policy areas as well as on their interdependencies, explaining their causal relationships. For example, Feindt, when using the ACF in the analysis of the EU CAP (policy system 1), demonstrated that the policy change that took place between 1970 and 2000 was related to the Environmental Policy Integration (policy system 2 [Feindt 2010]).

The ACF's distinction between *nascent* and *mature* subsystems and the process of transformation from one to the other can provide further insights. This is of particular use in situations when short-term analysis is not able to explain changes owing to its lack of a mid- or long-term perspective. This could be done also with longer horizons in institutional or multi-level governance studies. But, the ACF takes additional elements into consideration: not only the passage of time is factored in, but also changes in the context in which policies were created. For instance, Füg argued that the European agricultural policy came about as a result of a combination of strategic endeavours of coalitions and external developments. The outbreak of Bovine Spongiform Encephalopathy (BSE) in mainland Europe in November 2000 and the rekindling of World Trade Organization (WTO) negotiations on agriculture following the failure of the 1999 round in Seattle both presented important external events urging adaptation also at the EU level (Füg 2009: 6–7).

The focus on beliefs, values and the often overlooked factor of time in shaping EU policy styles (see, for example, Goetz and Meyer-Sahling 2009) and outputs provides a valuable perspective on processes taking place during EU policy development. Similar to the governance approach, it helps us to understand the EU multi-level character and how to handle diversified EU governance regimes. But, the ACF is better suited to clearly indicate how new idea sets can emerge in the EU system through the introduction of a group of actors devoted to a new paradigm (Dudley and Richardson 1996). It can be used to explain how change occurs during a period of crisis in a given policy area, when competing advocacy groups form a 'grand coalition' to change an unacceptable *status quo* (Dudley and Richardson 1999). Or, as Nedergaard suggested in the CAP study (Nedergraad 2008), the change can be brought about by a reversal in the majority coalition status. In a particular example of the CAP, the dominant agricultural coalition shifted its position with previously undecided, moderate reform coalition.

The EU, in terms of the ACF, can be characterized as a highly complex system, which shows characteristics of both *issue* and *institutional* complexity. *Issue* complexity refers to the amount and nature of informational linkages between actors in the system and may be operationalized as the degree of information overload (Zahariadis 2013). One of the EU characteristics is the large level of information flows between numerous actors, both individuals and groups (Chalmers 2011); thus, it fits the definition. In the ACF in particular, attention is given to the information flows between the members of a coalition. The exchange between these actors is posited to be permanent and rather nonconflicting, as actors share the same belief systems. They agree with regard to the identifications of problems and solutions. Information exchange seems to play a crucial role in creating and sustaining coalitions.

With regard to the information flow between coalitions, the situation is the opposite. Owing to the different *policy core* beliefs held by different coalitions, it is very rare that information flows between them. As Sabatier argues, such exchange could be primed only by severe external shocks and requires the willingness of the actors in each coalition to co-operate and look for a satisfactory consensus (Sabatier 1998). For instance, Quaglia provided evidence that the problem with the establishment of the EU single market in financial services was caused (among other reasons) by a division between a 'market-making' coalition and a 'market-shaping' one (Quaglia 2010). The division was caused by tensions between different belief systems (ideas) about financial services regulation and a lack of exchanges between coalitions on possible compromise solutions. The latter have only undergone a significant review as a result of a severe external shock (2008 global financial crisis).

At the moment there are several studies dealing with the EU issue complexity as defined by the ACF. Chalmers argues that information is currency for lobbying in the EU (Chalmers 2011). Similar argumentation can be found also in articles by Bouwen, Eising and Coen (Bouwen and McCown 2007; Coen 1997; Eising 2009). Influence and participation in coalitions is measured as a function of the actor's ability to efficiently transform and transmit information. Heaney demonstrates that information is a major element influencing coalition formation between actors in the EU (Heaney 2004). From Crombez's research it can be concluded that information overflow between coalitions has a different character at different stages of the EU policy-making (Crombez 2002). At the proposal stage, information flows mostly between members of the same coalition. At the voting stage, the flow is addressed mostly towards the 'pivotal' policy-maker (Crombez 2002: 28).

A large part of the ACF studies on the EU political system is devoted to the study of interest groups' participation in advocacy coalitions and their influence on policy outcomes. In the relatively complex and omni-directional dynamic of EU politics (Tsebelis and Garrett 2001), it is increasingly difficult to analytically and empirically assess interest group participation (Dür and De Bievre 2007). Focusing on complex, divergent political context, the advocacy coalition framework helps to complement the analysis of EU interest groups activity that is based on models which prioritize rational choice and resource dependency. The ACF adds the focus on context of the political system in which groups are active, and their position with regard to other participants in the system.

The interest group studies based in the ACF focus on few questions: the knowledge groups have of potential allies and adversaries in their environment (Heinz *et al.* 1993); why interest organizations become members of the coalitions (Hojnacki 1997); the extent to which membership of a coalition is a response to scarce resources (Gray and Lowery 1998); the roles that groups choose to play in coalitions (Hula 1999); and the importance of a group's reputation in determining its behaviour in a coalition (Hojnacki 1998). Those studies summarize that coalition membership is likely to positively influence the strength of the opinion voiced by the group to alter a legislative act.

There is, however, a dissonance in the results of those studies. While some authors suggest that coalition-forming is an effect of long-standing partnerships between organizations working on similar issues (Gueguen 2007; Mazey and

Richardson 2007; Pesendorfer 2006: 97), others provide evidence that the EU interest groups form or participate in short-term, *ad hoc* coalitions (Pijnenburg 1998; Warleigh 2000).

Szarka's analysis of the EU wind power sector provides the example for long-term coalitions in the EU political system. He applied the advocacy coalition framework to the wind power sector and linked coalition preferences to the choices of policy instruments made by policy-makers (Szarka 2010). On the one hand, the patterns of coalition behaviour have displayed stability over time, confirming the ACF's hypothesis that on major controversies within a policy subsystem (when policy core beliefs are in dispute) the line-up of allies and opponents tends to be rather stable over periods of a decade or so. Other features of the wind coalitions that corresponded to ACF expectations were the wide range of actors, the salience of beliefs and the occurrence of policy conflicts between coalitions at the subsystem level. On the other hand, the alliance of pro-environmental NGOs with energy producers was untypical of the ACF line-up found in previous analyses of environmental and energy policy, where one category tended to oppose the other. The author provided support for the advocacy coalition framework, but argued that its explanatory power can be increased by bringing both self-interest and public interest back into the analytical frame. In a similar way, Dudley and Richardson described and analysed the process of formulating EU steel policy over a 50-year period. They have conceptualized the process in terms of shifts in the balance of power in European steel policy which enabled a new policy frame to emerge (Dudley and Richardson 1999).

In contrast, there is a number of authors providing evidence of only short-term, *ad hoc* coalitions existing between the EU interest groups and interest groups and other stakeholders. Those *ad hoc* coalitions exist for a specific purpose: working on a single issue and dissolving when that issue is resolved or when the coalition partners no longer feel the effort is worthwhile (Pijnenburg 1998: 305). They are characterized by little or no formalization, limited duration, considerable autonomy of coalition partners, and a single issue profile. It has been argued that those types of coalitions are better equipped to deal with the EU dynamic environment and issue arenas. As *ad hoc* coalitions are focused on one specific issue, it is easier to outline common interests at stake for the actors involved. As collective action taken by members of the coalition is on a smaller and short-term scale, the ACF perspective of a decade or so becomes irrelevant. *Ad hoc* coalitions are flexible and are less inhabited (number of actors is lower than in the stable advocacy coalitions), thus there is more room for manoeuvre when it comes to exercising influence in less stable political systems, which are prone to rapid changes (Pijnenburg 1998: 307). The ACF posits that coalition actors engage in some nontrivial degree of co-ordinated activity in pursuit of common policy objectives (Sabatier and Jenkins-Smith 1999: 127). Because joint action in the ACF is strategic, the time frame is long, unlike in the *ad hoc* coalitions, where coalition behaviour is temporary and tactical (Szarka 2010: 837).

In the EU studies, one of the best illustrative examples is Warleigh's work. He analysed the lobbying undertaken by non-governmental organizations in the auto oil, drinking water and unit pricing directives in order to establish whether such organizations can affect public policy outcomes (Warleigh 2000). He argued that such is in fact the case, but that lobbying success depends on membership of fast-changing and issue-specific alliances usually constructed on an *ad hoc* basis – policy coalitions. He set up a model of the latter, contrasting it with Sabatier's model of the advocacy coalitions which appears unable to entirely encapsulate the entrepreneurial dynamics of EU decision-making. Similar evidence and conclusions were delivered by Pijnenburg (Pijnenburg 1998). He summed up that, when successful, the EU interest group coalitions are usually short term rather than oriented towards the long-time perspective, and motivated by complementary immediate goals rather than a common world-view or development agenda.

Several authors point out that EU interest groups normally prioritize short-term goals over long-standing interests and are prepared to 'think outside the box' by forging useful alliances wherever they can be found (see, for example, Warleigh 2000: 238). The evidence generated by the past research points to high level of resource dependency and interest groups' success (Crombez 2002; Gerber 1999; Kohler-Koch 1994). Money is interpreted as one of the most influential resource (Crombez 2002; Hall and Deardorff 2006). It is followed by knowledge, expertise and information, which are interpreted as 'access goods' (Bouwen 2002; Immergut 1992), and further supplemented by groups' structural characteristics: size, type of membership (Gerber 1999); internal organization and geographical concentration (McLaughlin *et al.* 1993: 200). The majority of studies show that groups with broad-based support and significant organizational resources (larger staff, offices based in strategic points) have proven to be extremely effective in realizing their objectives. While being part of a coalition has merits, it seems that in the EU arena other resources are of larger importance.

Coalitions do exist in the EU political system. Indeed they are crucial for EU policy-making, given the complexity of the system and its multiple arenas and dimensions. There is an institutionally generated need for co-operation between actors. Relationships within a policy coalition can be strong, given a great degree of interdependence between actors in a coalition. Nonetheless, it seems that the EU interest groups' primary rationale for developing policy coalitions is not long-standing common interests based on common value (belief) system, as in the ACF, but rather the chaotic, unorganized seeking of policy goals which will provide win–win result for all members of the coalition. In the entrepreneurial and evolving climate of EU political environment, achieving policy goals is more important to EU actors than adhering to established patterns of alliance.

DISSCUSSION AND CONCLUSIONS

The advocacy coalition framework can be considered one of the most promising frameworks to explain the EU policy processes. It helps to organize thinking about EU public policies. It points to the importance of studying the context of the system that prompted change. Its ability to deal with complex situations and its focus on belief systems make it an interesting alternative to the institutional rational choice models. However, as Sabatier concluded himself (Sabatier 1998: 121), the ACF only points to certain relationships or processes as being important, but it does not give all the answers with regard to the EU policy processes. The dynamics of EU interest groups activities cannot be single-handedly encapsulated by Sabatier's framework. The ACF cannot clearly explain the patterns of interest representation and alliance construction at the EU level. The opportunistic search for policy gains by EU interest groups in a fast-moving political system decreases the ACF explanatory power.

In order to be better applicable to the EU *fluid* environment, the framework needs to be combined with other theoretical approaches (see also Füg 2009: 4). Those approaches have to address, in particular, the ACF problems with the EU dynamic policy change, cross-learning between coalitions, and tentative coalitions that are so characteristic to the EU political system. The policy entrepreneurship model, against the ACF stability, can explain dynamic policy change. In that interpretation, a change in policy processes can be caused by a skilful entrepreneur who is part of a coalition. The skilful actor can not only introduce an exogenous event into the coalition, but also, by framing policy information consolidate a coalition (Mintrom and Vergari 1996: 431; Zahariadis 2008: 521). The inclusion of policy narratives in the framework could further improve the analysis of cognitive variables and policy change (Radaelli 1999: 662). Analysing the EU political system from the perspective of framing could allow for a re-examination of Sabatier's argument that the policy core is relatively impenetrable to learning. The argument would be that a narrative developed in the absence of solid empirical evidence can also be a catalyst of a change (Radaelli 1999: 679). Another improvement of the ACF could come from a deeper study of the interdependencies between actors in the coalitions. Major theoretical frameworks to draw on could be the network and the resource-dependency theories (Fenger and Klok 2001: 169). The idea is not to replace the theoretical core of the ACF, which is based on beliefs, but rather to consider that actors are building coalitions based not only on their beliefs but also shared interests and owing to their interdependencies (Börzel 1997: 5; Kenis and Schneider 1991: 44; Schneider 1988).

The insights that can be provided by other theoretical approaches are useful; however, they also show that there are still open questions in theory-driven empirical studies of EU policy coalitions. While the ACF deals well with the analysis of long-term changes in a political system, there is a lack of comparative studies between several policy areas. In particular in EU studies, the comparative element could have an added value. Also, membership of coalitions is a rather unexplored area in studies based in the ACF. It is still unclear how stable the membership of coalitions is, how many actors are in coalitions at a given time, if membership is dependent on the salience of the policy at stake, and, finally, if there are any observable membership patterns. The added value would be also a study of EU coalitions after the conclusion of the dossier which prompted the formation of the coalitions. It could allow for falsification or endorsement of the claim that choice of partners is issue-specific rather than habitual, in that no coalition is recreated without significant differences in membership.

Biographical note: Patrycja Rozbicka is a post-doc at the Ruhr University Bochum, Germany, primarily involved with the INTEREURO Project.

ACKNOWLEDGEMENTS

I wish to thank Nikolaos Zahariadis and the anonymous reviewers for their helpful comments on early drafts.

REFERENCES

Ainsworth, S. (2001) 'Lobbying together: interest group coalitions in legislative politics', *American Political Science Review* 95: 475–75.
Bouwen, P. (2002) 'Corporate lobbying in the European Union: the logic of access', *Journal of European Public Policy* 9: 365–90.
Bouwen, P. and McCown, M. (2007) 'Lobbying versus litigation: political and legal strategies of interest representation in the European Union', *Journal of European Public Policy* 14: 422–43.
Börzel, T.A. (1997) 'What's so special about policy networks? An exploration of the concept and its usefulness in studying European governance', *European Integration online Papers (EIoP) 1*, available at http://eiop.or.at/eiop/texte/1997-016a.htm (accessed 4 April 2013).
Chalmers, A.W. (2011) 'Interests, influence and information: comparing the influence of interest groups in the European Union', *Journal of European Integration* 33: 471–86.
Chalmers, A.W. (2011) 'Interests, influence and information: comparing the influence of interest groups in the European Union', *Journal of European Integration* 33: 471–86.
Coen, D. (1997) 'The evolution of the large firm as a political actor in the European Union', *Journal of European Public Policy* 4: 91–108.
Cram, L. (2001) 'Integration theory and the study of the European policy process', in J. Richardson (ed.), *European Union: Power and Policy-Making*, London: Routledge, pp. 51–73.
Crombez, Ch. (2002) 'Information, lobbying and the legislative process in the European Union', *European Union Politics* 3: 7–32.

Daviter, F. (2007) 'Policy framing in the European Union', *Journal of European Public Policy* 14: 654–66.

Daviter, F. (2009) 'Schattschneider in Brussels: how policy conflict reshaped the biotechnology agenda in the European Union', *West European Politics* 32: 1118–39.

Dudley, G. and Richardson, J. (1996) 'Why does policy change over time? Adversarial policy communities, alternative policy arenas, and British trunk roads policy 1945–95', *Journal of European Public Policy* 3: 63–83.

Dudley, G. and Richardson, J. (1999) 'Competing advocacy coalitions and the process of "frame reflection": a longitudinal analysis of EU steel policy', *Journal of European Public Policy* 6: 225–48.

Dür, A. and De Bievre, D. (2007) 'The question of interest group influence', *Journal of Public Policy* 27: 1–12.

Eising, R. (2009) *The Political Economy of State-Business Relations in Europe : Interest Mediation, Capitalism and Eu Policy Making*, New York: Routledge.

Eising, R. and Kohler-Koch, B. (1999) 'Introduction: network governance in the European Union', in R. Eising and B. Kohler-Koch (eds), *The Transformation of Governance in the European Union*, London: Routledge, pp. 3–14.

Feindt, P.H. (2010) 'Policy-learning and environmental policy integration in the Common Agricultural Policy, 1973–2003', *Public Administration* 88: 296–314.

Fenger, M. and Klok, P.-J. (2001) 'Interdependency, beliefs, and coalition behavior: a contribution to the advocacy coalition framework', *Policy Sciences* 34: 157–70.

Füg, O.C. (2009). 'The advocacy coalition framework goes to Europe. An American theory and its application across the pond'. Paper for the *Annual Convention of Political Science Studies Assosiation. Panel 115: Advocacy Coalitions and Democracy in Europe I*, Manchaster, 7–9 April.

Gerber, E.R. (1999) *The Populist Paradox: Interest Group Influence and the Promise of Direct Legislation*, Princeton, NJ: Princeton University Press.

Goetz, K.H. and Meyer-Sahling, J.-H. (2009) 'Political time in the EU: dimensions, perspectives, theories', *Journal of European Public Policy* 16: 180–201.

Gray, V. and Lowery, D. (1998) 'To lobby alone or in a flock', *American Politics Research* 26: 5–34.

Gueguen, D. (2007) *European Lobbying*, 2nd edn, Brussels: Europolitics.

Hall, R.L. and Deardorff, A. (2006) 'Lobbying as legislative subsidy', *American Political Science Review* 100: 69–84.

Heaney, M.T. (2004) 'Issue networks, information, and interest group alliances: the case of Wisconsin welfare politics, 1993–99', *State Politics & Policy Quarterly* 4: 237–70.

Heinz, J.P., Laumann, E.O., Nelson, R.L. and Salisbury, R.H. (1993) *The Hollow Core : Private Interests in National Policy Making*, London: Harvard University Press.

Hojnacki, M. (1997) 'Interest groups' decisions to join alliances or work alone', *American Journal of Political SCience* 41: 61–87.

Hojnacki, M. (1998) 'Organized interests' advocacy behavior in alliances', *Political Research Quarterly* 51: 437–59.

Hooghe, L. and Marks, G. (2001) *Multi-Level Governance and European Integration*, Lanham, MD: Rowman & Littlefield.

Hosli, M.O., Nölke, A. and Beyers, J. (2004) 'Contending political-economy perspectives on European interest group activity', in A. Wonka and A. Warntjen (eds), *Governance in the EU. The Role of of Interest Groups*, Baden-Baden: Nomos Verlagsgesellschaft, pp. 42–56.

Hula, K.W. (1999) *Lobbying Together : Interest Group Coalitions in Legislative Politics*, Washington, DC: Georgetown University Press.

Immergut, H. (1992) *Health Politics: Interests and Institutions in Western Europe*, Cambridge: Cambridge University Press.

Kenis, M. and Schneider, V. (1991) 'Policy networks and policy analysis: scrutinizing a new analytical toolbox', in B. Marin and R. Mayntz (eds), *Policy Network: Empirical Evidence and Theoretical Considerations*, Frankfurt aM: Campus Verlag, pp. 25–59.

Knodt, M., Greenwood, J. and Quittkat, Ch. (2011) 'Territorial and functional interest representation in EU governance', *Journal of European Integration* 33: 349–67.

Kohler-Koch, B. (1994) 'Changing patterns of interest intermediation in the European Union', *Government and Opposition* 29: 166–80.

Marks, G. (1993) 'Structural policy and multi-level governance in the EC', in A. Cafruny and G. Rosenthal (eds), *The State of the European Community*, London: Longman, pp. 391–409.

Marks, G., Hooghe, L. and Blank, K. (1996) 'European integration from the 1980s: state-centric v. multi-level governance', *Journal of Common Market Studies* 34: 341–78.

Mazey, S. (1998) 'The European Union and women's rights: from the Europeanization of national agendas to the nationalization of a European agenda?', *Journal of European Public Policy* 5: 131–52.

Mazey, S. and Richardson, J. (2007) 'Environmental groups and the EC: challenges and opportunities', in A. Jordan (ed.), *Environmental Policy in the European Union. Actors, Institutions & Processes*, London: Earthscan, pp. 106–24.

McLaughlin, A.M., Jordan, G. and Maloney, W.A. (1993) 'Corporate lobbying in the European Community', *Journal of Common Market Studies* 31: 191–212.

Mintrom, M. and Vergari, S. (1996) 'Advocacy coalitions, policy entrepreneurs, and policy change', *Policy Studies Journal* 24: 420–34.

Moravcsik, A. (1998) *The Choice for Europe*, Ithaca, NY, and London: Cornell University Press and ICL Press.

Nedergraad, P. (2008) 'The reform of the 2003 Common Agricultural Policy: an advocacy coalition explanation', *Policy Studies* 29(2): 179–95.

Pesendorfer, D. (2006) 'EU environmental policy under pressure: chemicals policy change between antagonistic goals?', *Environmental Politics* 15: 95–114.

Peterson, J. (1995) 'Decision-making in the European Union: towards a framework for analysis', *Journal of European Public Policy* 2: 69–93.

Pijnenburg, B. (1998) 'EU lobbying by ad hoc coalitions: an exploratory case study', *Journal of European Public Policy* 5: 303–21.

Pollack, M.A. (2005) 'Theorizing EU policy-making', in W. Wallece and M.A. Pollack (eds), *Policy-Making in the European Union*, Oxford: Oxford University Press, pp. 13–48.

Quaglia, L. (2010) 'Completing the single market in financial services: the politics of competing advocacy coalitions', *Journal of European Public Policy* 17: 1007–23.

Radaelli, C.M. (1999) 'Harmful tax competition in the EU: policy narratives and advocacy coalitions', *Journal of Common Market Studies* 37: 661–82.

Roe, E. (1994) *Narrative Policy Analysis: Theory and Practice*, Durham, NC: Duke University Press.

Sabatier, P.A. (1988) 'An advocacy coalition framework of policy change and the role of policy-oriented learning therein', *Policy Sciences* 21: 129–68.

Sabatier, P.A. (1993) 'Policy change over a decade or more', in P. Sabatier and H. Jenkins-Smith (eds), *Policy Change and Learning, an Advocacy Coalition Approach*, Boulder, CO: Westview Press, pp. 13–39.

Sabatier, P.A. (1998) 'The advocacy coalition framework: revisions and relevance for Europe', *Journal of European Public Policy* 5: 98–130.

Sabatier, P.A. and Jenkins-Smith, H. (1993) 'The advocacy coalition framework: assesment, revisions, and implications for scholars and practicioners', in P. Sabatier and H. Jenkins-Smith (eds), *Policy Change and Learning: An Advocacy Coalition Approach*, Boulder, CO: Westview Press, pp. 211–35.

Sabatier, P.A. and Jenkins-Smith, H.C. (1999) 'The advocacy coalition framework: an assessment', in P.A. Sabatier (ed.), *Theories of the Policy Process*, Boulder, CO: Westview Press, pp. 117–68.

Sabatier, P.A. and Zafonte, M. (1997) 'Are bureaucrats and scientists members of advocacy coalitions? Evidence from an intergovernmental water policy subsystem', in P. Sabatier (ed.), *An Advocacy Coalition Lens on Environmental Policy*, unpublished manuscript.

Schlager, E. (1995) 'Policy making and collective action: defining coalitions within the advocacy coalition framework', *Policy Sciences* 28: 243–70.

Schmitter, C.P. (2002) 'Participation in governance arrangements: is there any reason to expect it will achieve sustainable and innovative policies in a multilevel context?', in J.R.Grote and B. Gbikpi (eds), *Participatory Governance. Political and Societal Implications*, Opladen: Leske+Budrich, pp. 51–70.

Schneider, V. (1988) *Politiknetzwerke Der Chemikalienkontrolle. Ein Analyse Einer Transnationalen Politikentwicklung*, Berlin: de Gruyter.

Shanahan, E.A., Jones, M.D. and McBeth, M.K. (2011) 'Policy narratives and policy processes', *Policy Studies Journal* 39(3): 535–61.

Szarka, J. (2010) 'Bringing interest back in: using coalition theories to explain European winf power policies', *Journal of Europen Public Policy* 17(6): 836–53.

Tsebelis, G. and Garrett, G. (2001) 'The institutional foundations of intergovernmentalism and supranationalism in the European Union', *International Organization* 55: 357–90.

Warleigh, A. (2000) 'The hustle: citizenship practice, NGOs and policy coalitions in the European Union – the cases of auto oil, drinking water and unit pricing', *Journal of European Public Policy* 7: 229–43.

Weible, Ch.M. (2006) 'An advocacy coalition framework approach to stakeholder analysis: understanding the political context of California marine protected area policy', *Journal of Public Administration Research and Theory* 17: 95–117.

Weible, Ch.M., Sabatier, P.A. and Flowers, J. (2008) 'Advocacy coalition framework', in E.M. Berman (ed.), *Encyclopedia of Public Administration and Public Policy*, Vol. 1, 2nd edn, London: Taylor & Francis, pp. 1–10.

Weible, Ch.M., Sabatier, P.A. and McQueen, K. (2009) 'Themes and variations: taking stock of the advocacy coalition framework', *The Policy Studies Journal* 37(1): 121–40.

Zahariadis, N. (2008) 'Ambiguity and choice in European public policy', *Journal of European Public Policy* 15(4): 514–30.

Zahariadis, N. (2013) 'Building better theoretical frameworks of the European Union's policy process', *Journal of European Public Policy* 20(6), doi: 10.1080/13501763.2013.781815.

Punctuated equilibrium theory and the European Union

Sebastiaan Princen

ABSTRACT   This contribution discusses punctuated equilibrium theory (PET) and its application to European Union (EU) policy processes. It argues that PET includes two approaches, one that relies on case studies of individual issues and one that analyses overall distributions of policy change. Whereas the former approach has gained a strong foothold in studies of EU policy-making, application of the latter to the EU is still in its infancy. Because of its focus on the allocation of attention and the interplay of institutional and ideational factors, PET is well-suited to deal with the institutional and issue complexity inherent in EU policy-making. However, for this potential to be realized, PET needs to be applied to EU policy-making in a more systematic way than has so far been the case. This, in turn, has the potential to contribute to the further development of PET, as the EU offers a fertile testing ground for several outstanding issues in the theory.

1.   INTRODUCTION

Since the early 1990s, punctuated equilibrium theory (PET) has established itself as one of the leading theories of the policy process. Initially, PET sought to explain a specific pattern of policy change, in which long periods of stability and incremental change are 'punctuated' by outbursts of policy activity and radical change. From this initial observation, PET has developed into a much more general theory of policy-making, which focuses on the allocation of attention and disproportionate information processing as the key explanatory variables.

PET starts from the observation that policy-making is often characterized by a dual pattern of long periods of stability, punctuated by brief episodes of radical change (Baumgartner and Jones 1993; True *et al.* 2007: 155). After such a radical change, policy-making will revert to a situation of equilibrium again, albeit a different equilibrium than the one that existed before the change. A basic contention of PET is that equilibrium and change are both part of the same process of policy-making and derive from the same policy dynamics. Thus, instances of radical change should not be treated as 'flukes', exceptions or outliers, but should be seen as an inherent part of the policy-making process.

In explaining this pattern of stability-with-radical-change, PET accords a central place to the concept of attention, thus building on the agenda-setting literature, in particular the work by Schattschneider (1960), Cobb and Elder (1972) and Kingdon (2003). Policy-makers have limited attention spans. As a result, they can only deal with a limited set of issues (or aspects of issues) at a time, while ignoring other issues. These cognitive limitations are reinforced by institutional factors. Modern governments are organized along functional lines, in which each organization or unit is responsible for a specific task, value or objective. Hence, governmental organizations are 'programmed' to focus on a limited set of issues and to ignore others. As a result, they are slow to respond to (signals about) developments that lie outside of their institutional remit. Combined with the cognitive limitations of policy-makers, this leads to stability and incremental policy-making.

This pattern is broken when attention shifts from one (aspect of an) issue to another. This may occur because of a large-scale focusing event (cf. Kingdon 2003), which draws attention to a hitherto ignored problem, or because the pressure on a policy programme reaches some threshold level above which it can no longer be ignored. If that happens, an established policy programme is seen in an entirely different light and radical changes in policy may take place. Because these changes address issues that were previously ignored, they tend to make up for lost time, as it were, by instituting a radical change in policy.

According to PET, then, stability and policy change are not two different processes, but two sides of the same coin. Radical shifts occur *because* some issues and negative consequences of existing policies are ignored in periods of policy stability. And policy change will be more radical to the extent that issues and problems have been ignored for a longer time.

Because of the way PET integrates institutions, information-processing and attention in one theoretical framework, it is well suited to deal with (and to some extent even assumes) situations of high institutional and issue complexity (cf. Zahariadis, 2013). High institutional complexity implies the existence of many interconnected policy-making venues. As will be argued below, this increases the potential for both stasis and radical change. In addition, high issue complexity leads to incomplete, contested and ambiguous information, which increases the importance of framing and the allocation of attention to various aspects of an issue.

Within PET, two types of studies can be discerned, which build on Baumgartner and Jones's earlier and later work, respectively. The first type uses (comparative) case studies to analyse policy dynamics around specific issues. The second type relies on analyses of change distributions across a wide range of issues. In the next section, I introduce these two strands in the PET literature. Then, I turn to the application of PET to studies of EU policy-making. In the final section, I discuss the strengths and weaknesses of the current use of PET in EU policy studies and outline an agenda for research.

2. THE VARIETIES OF PUNCTUATED EQUILIBRIUM THEORY

2.1. The case study approach in punctuated equilibrium theory

The case study approach to PET goes back to the early work of Baumgartner and Jones (1991, 1993), exemplified by their 1993 book *Agendas and Instability in American Politics*. It uses PET to explain specific cases of policy-making and relies on case studies of individual issues.

Central concepts in this approach are 'venues' and 'policy images'. Venues are the institutional loci where authoritative decisions on a given policy are taken (Baumgartner and Jones 1993: 32). In normal circumstances, policy-making takes place in venues that are formed by relatively closed circles of experts on a given issue, so-called 'policy subsystems'. Policy subsystems deal with an issue on the basis of existing policies. As a result, they tend to maintain the *status quo*. For instance, the mission of a competition authority is to safeguard competition on the basis of existing competition law. As a result, its activities will be focused on that objective, and it will tend to ignore other objectives, such as environmental protection, consumer protection or worker rights. This holds true not just for the competition authority, but for all venues that deal with the issue of competition policy on a routine basis, such as parliamentary committees or governmental policy departments devoted to competition issues.

The assignment of a policy issue to a given subsystem is underpinned by a dominant 'policy image', which consists of the way in which a policy and the problems it is supposed to address are framed (Baumgartner and Jones 1993: 25ff.). For instance, competition policy is premised on the assumptions that (1) free competition is the best way to ensure economic efficiency and (2) left to their own devices firms will tend to undermine free competition through cartels and concentrations.

As long as policy-making takes place within (the venues of) a policy subsystem, the basic presumptions underlying existing policies will be taken for granted and policy change will not take place or be limited to minor aspects of the policy. Signals that are irrelevant to or contradictory to existing policies will be ignored, thus reinforcing the *status quo* and leading to incrementalist patterns of policy-making. In PET, this process is known as 'negative feedback': the 'dampening' of signals that do not fit the dominant set of policies exemplified by the combination of existing venues and dominant policy images (True *et al.* 2007: 160).

This changes when an issue is picked up by another venue that takes a very different stance towards the issue. When, for instance, mergers between firms are not viewed from the perspective of competition policy but from the perspective of foreign policy (for instance, on the theory that it is necessary to create 'national champions' in order to withstand foreign access to vital technologies), an entirely different set of considerations enters the debate. This may lead to a fundamental reconsideration of the prevailing assumptions underlying existing policies (such as the idea that a dominant position of a single firm on a market is bad for the economy).

Hence, a shift in the venue that takes decisions on a policy will increase the likelihood that that policy will undergo radical change. For this reason, actors that are opposed to the *status quo* may actively engage in attempts to shift policy-making from one venue to another venue. In PET, this is known as 'venue-shopping': active attempts by an actor to involve other venues that are more favourable to the actor's point of view than venues in the existing policy subsystem (Baumgartner and Jones 1993: 36). Often, a change in policy image is a crucial precondition for a change in venue, because the allocation of an issue to a venue is underpinned by a policy image that justifies that allocation. Changing the definition of an issue (that is, the policy image) therefore often implies a shift in the venue that deals with it. If, for instance, healthcare is defined as a social issue (how to give the best care to the greatest number of patients) it will be dealt with by health policy experts. If, by contrast, it is defined primarily as a financial issue (because of the burden healthcare expenditures place on the government budget), it will more readily be taken up by financial policy experts. This is why battles over the definition of issues and shifts in dominant policy images often precede shifts in venues (and the associated sets of policies).

Shifts in image and venue reinforce each other. Once a dominant policy image is challenged, other venues will become active on that issue. And once those other venues become active, they will contribute to a further redefinition of the issue. This process is known as 'positive feedback', and it may lead to a rapid, 'cascading' policy change once the dominant policy arrangements have been challenged.

The focus on interest groups and a plurality of political venues betrays PET's origins in the United States (US) political system. However, a similar logic can be applied to political systems with other characteristics. For instance, on the basis of the PET approach, Christoffer Green-Pedersen and collaborators have shown that party competition is an important driver of governmental attention and policy change in European political systems with fewer venues, thus confirming the applicability of PET beyond the US (Albaek *et al.* 2007; Green-Pedersen 2007; Green-Pedersen and Krogstrup 2008).

2.2. Analysing change distributions in punctuated equilibrium theory

The second strand in the PET literature builds on the later work by Baumgartner and Jones, which comes out most clearly in their book *The Politics of Attention* (Jones and Baumgartner 2005). This strand of literature does not seek to explain individual cases but overall distributions of policy change. This approach therefore shifts attempts to explain policy change away from individual cases to overall patterns of change.

Change distributions offer an opportunity to examine patterns of punctuated equilibrium across a large number of issues in a political system or venue as a whole. Compared to non-punctuated change distributions, distributions that are characterized by punctuated equilibrium will have (1) relatively many cases of no or little change (reflecting the periods of stability) and (2) relatively many cases of radical (i.e., extreme) policy change (reflecting the punctuations). By implication, the category of moderate change, which lies in between these two extremes, will be relatively less prevalent (True *et al.* 2007: 168).

Through the analysis of change distributions, punctuated equilibrium has been shown to be a characteristic of policy-making in a wide variety of contexts and political systems (e.g., Baumgartner *et al.* 2009; Jensen 2009; John and Margetts 2003; Jones *et al.* 2003; Mortensen 2005; Walgrave and Vliegenthart 2010). At the same time, differences can also be observed in the extent to which change distributions are punctuated. These differences are primarily explained in terms of the level of friction induced by institutions (Jones and Baumgartner 2005: 145ff.). As was noted above, cognitive and institutional limitations on information processing play a central role in PET. Assuming that cognitive limitations do not vary systematically between policy-makers in different political systems, differences between those systems are a result of differences in the level of friction that institutional frameworks impose on the policy-making process.

Friction occurs because institutional frameworks impose certain 'hurdles' for policy change, for instance by focusing attention away from signals that undermine existing policies or by imposing demanding decision-making requirements for policy decisions to be taken. To the extent that policy-making institutions impose such friction, policy change will be less frequent (leading to longer periods of stability) but once it comes the 'correction' will be greater (leading to larger punctuations). Thus, in a comparative study of change distributions in a range of US policy-making institutions, Jones *et al.* (2003) found differences in degrees of punctuation that were predictable in terms of the level of friction these institutions imposed. This finding was confirmed in a comparative study of policy-making institutions in Belgium, Denmark and the US (Baumgartner *et al.* 2009). Both studies found that change distributions became more punctuated as issues moved from the early stages of the policy process (media attention, election outcomes, parliamentary questions) to later stages (budgets and legislation). This can be explained by an increase of friction during the process, as the hurdles that need to be overcome before a decision can be taken become higher.

The effects of friction are reinforced by the operation of cascades (Jones and Baumgartner 2005: 140–2). Cascades occur when actors mimic each other's behaviour. Then, large numbers of actors may rapidly turn their attention to a given issue once a sufficient number of (influential) actors do so. For instance, newspapers tend to report on issues on which other media outlets also report, since they are constantly monitoring each other's reporting. As a result, issues can quickly 'explode' and turn into media hypes. Comparing attention for issues in the media and parliament in Belgium, Walgrave and Vliegenthart (2010) showed that media reporting is more likely to be affected by cascades and parliamentary attention by friction, although in both cases the pattern of attention shifts is explained by a combination of cascades and friction.

Analysis of change distributions requires quantitative data on policy change. To this end, a standardized coding scheme has been developed (see http://www. comparativeagendas.info). The coding scheme discerns 19 major topics, ranging from 'macroeconomics' to 'community development and housing' and from 'energy' to 'foreign trade'. These major topics contain a total of 225 subtopics that define more specific issues. For instance, major topic 1 (macroeconomics) contains nine subtopics, such as 'inflation, prices, and interest rates', 'unemployment rate' and 'taxation, tax policy, and tax reform'. This standardized set of subtopic codes can be (and has been) applied to a wide range of policy outputs, such as legislation, budgetary outlays, parliamentary questions, hearings, executive speeches, media coverage and public opinion polls. In this way, the attention for issues, and changes in attention between time periods, can be systematically assessed. The existence of punctuated change distributions and the extent to which those distributions are punctuated can be assessed statistically and expressed in a statistical measure (L-kurtosis), allowing for rigorous comparisons between political systems and types of policy outputs.

Although the focus on change distributions has yielded many important insights about policy-making processes, it has come at the cost of obscuring the underlying substantive policy issues, which are central to the case-study-based approach in PET. A potential bridge between these two approaches in PET can be found in case study applications of the large-scale datasets compiled with a view to analysing change distributions. Since these datasets have been created on the basis of a common coding scheme, they can be used to compare attention for different issues in a political system or for the same issues between political systems and over time. In this vein, Green-Pedersen and Wilkerson (2006) and Green-Pedersen and Wolfe (2009) have compared attention for health and environmental issues respectively in Denmark and the United States.

3. PUNCTUATED EQUILIBRIUM THEORY IN STUDIES OF EU POLICY-MAKING

3.1. Venues and frames in the EU

Using the distinction between the two strands of PET made above, two types of applications to the EU can be discerned. Of these two types, the approach that builds on the dynamics of venues and policy images has gained most ground in studies of EU policy-making. The concept of 'venue-shopping', in particular, has gained considerable currency in studies of the EU. This is not surprising, since the EU seems ideally suited for an analysis in terms of venues and venue-shopping, both because the EU as a whole can be conceptualized as a venue and because the EU itself is characterized by the existence of multiple venues. This leads to two types of venue-shopping: from the member states to the European Union ('vertical venue-shopping') and between different venues at the EU level ('horizontal venue-shopping') (Princen 2009: 28).

In processes of vertical venue-shopping, the EU can be conceptualized as a policy-making venue alongside national (and subnational) venues in the member states, as well as global venues beyond the EU. The key question then becomes how and under what conditions political actors try and are able to move an issue from a domestic venue to the EU. This question ties in with a longstanding interest among scholars of EU politics in the process of European integration; that is, the process through which the EU develops and acquires new tasks and competences.

Processes of vertical venue-shopping, in which new issues are placed on the EU agenda, are characterized by a dual challenge for prospective agenda-setters (Princen 2011). The first challenge is to gain the attention of policy-makers to their preferred issue and approach. This is no different from the challenge that actors face in other political systems. The second challenge is to build credibility for the EU as the locus of policy- and decision-making on that issue, rather than the member states themselves (or other international organizations, depending on the issue at hand). This challenge is specific to polities whose competences and roles are not completely crystallized and remain contested, as is the case with the EU in 'new' areas of policy-making.

Attempts by domestic political actors to bring (new) issues to the EU in order to find a more receptive ear for their claims have been widely documented. These are examples of venue-shopping *par excellence* and PET provides a convenient label for this phenomenon, as well as a description of the underlying dynamics and political rationale.

In this way, Virginie Guiraudon (2000) analysed the rationale behind the development of an EU immigration policy in the 1980s and 1990s. Her argument is that a 'venue-shopping framework' best explains the form, content and timing of this policy. Immigration policy officials from EU member states who favoured stricter measures to control immigration were confronted domestically with opposition from actors who favoured an approach that emphasized the rights of immigrants. As a result, the advocates of stricter measures created a number of policy-making venues at the European level that excluded the advocates of immigrant rights and were thus more favourable towards their claims. This, in turn, led to the adoption of a set of relatively restrictive immigration policies in the EU. To enable this move, the issue of migration was framed in terms of 'global threats demanding transnational responses' (Guiraudon 2000: 260), which justified the shift of policy-making authority from the member state to the EU level. This analysis rests on the venue-framing dynamic that forms the core of Baumgartner and Jones's early work.

Explanations in terms of venue-shopping can also be used when the EU institutions are the drivers behind bringing an issue to the EU level. In an analysis of the development of EU social policy, Bryan Wendon (1998) showed how the European Commission acted as an 'image-venue entrepreneur' by simultaneously crafting a new policy image built on a link between social policy and economic growth and building institutional venues at the EU level that could be used for policy-making on these issues. This analysis forms an important complement to conceptions of venue-shopping that tend to see the EU institutions as passive 'receivers' of claims from other political actors, such as interest groups or member state governments. Also, it shows that the conceptual and theoretical tools of PET can equally well be applied to activities of the EU institutions themselves.

In addition to viewing the EU as a venue *vis-à-vis* member states, the EU itself is characterized by the existence of a large number of potential policy-making venues. These are formed by the various EU institutions (Commission, Council, European Council and Parliament) as well as the subdivisions within them (such as the various Directorates-General [DGs] in the Commission). It has been a longstanding contention about the EU as a political system that it is characterized by a large number of access points (e.g. Guy Peters's [1994] pioneering work on agenda-setting in the EU). As a result, political actors face a wide choice as to the venues within the EU that they target in order to gain access to EU policy-making – a crucial precondition for venue-shopping to take place. Moreover, in the existence of multiple venues the EU resembles the US, the political system in which PET was originally developed (cf. Fabbrini 2003).

For policies that are well-established at the EU level, the key question is what drives change in their form and content over time. Venue-shopping will then take place between different venues at the EU level, a process that can be called 'horizontal venue-shopping'. In terms of PET, we may expect these processes of agenda-setting and policy change to resemble those in other pluralist political systems (such as the US).

This is borne out by studies that have analysed EU policy change from the perspective of PET. In a comparison of agricultural policy reform in the EU and the US during the 1990s, Adam Sheingate (2000) argued that liberalization of agricultural policy required similar strategies by reformers in both polities: the redefinition of agricultural subsidies in terms of the negative externalities associated with them; and the strategic exploitation of favourable venues. In this process, venue shifts are crucially mediated by the success in redefining the issue in terms of externalities.

In a study of another well-established EU policy area, Princen (2009, 2010) argued that the move towards an ecosystems approach to fisheries policy resulted from venue change induced by a redefinition of the issue. By redefining fisheries issues in terms of (threats to) biodiversity, environmental NGOs succeeded in involving environmental policy venues in fisheries policy-making, which introduced an entirely different set of actors, perspectives and policy instruments. Here, too, the 'classic' PET mechanism of mutually reinforcing image and venue shifts led to a fundamental reconsideration of the premises on which existing policies were built.

Processes of vertical and horizontal venue-shopping have also been studied in combination. In many cases, the EU is both an alternative venue for other (member state or global) venues and itself a set of alternative venues. Venue-shopping processes then involve both attempts to move a new issue onto the

EU agenda and the search for the most favourable venue within the EU. Thus, Richard Parrish's (2003) analysis of the political struggle around sports policy in the EU highlights both attempts to place sports on the EU agenda as a new issue and the existence of competing venues with different institutional foci at the EU level. This offered dual opportunities for political actors to shop for the most favourable venue by redefining the issue in terms of either internal market concerns or the socio-cultural aspects of sports. Similar processes of vertical-plus-horizontal venue-shopping have also been observed in other attempts to place issues on the EU agenda: for instance, in the fields of alcohol abuse and health systems (Princen 2009).

All examples above related to venue-shopping towards or at the EU level. In addition, political actors may also engage in venue-shopping from the EU toward the global level. An example of the latter is Chad Damro's (2006) study of venue-shopping by the European Commission's DG Competition among four international organizations in order to achieve co-ordination and convergence of global competition policy. Likewise, in the case of EU fisheries policy already highlighted above, an important driver of policy change within the EU was formed by (successful) attempts to involve global environmental venues, such as the United Nations (UN) General Assembly and the Convention on Biological Diversity (CBD), in fisheries policy issues. This pattern can also be observed in health policy, where organizations such as the World Health Organization (WHO), the World Trade Organization (WTO), the Organization for Economic Co-operation and Development (OECD) and the Council of Europe have variously been enlisted as sympathetic venues by opposing sides of policy debates in the EU (Princen 2009).

In addition to analyses that look at the venue-image dynamic typical of PET, some authors have zoomed in on one of the two central elements of the theory. For instance, Beyers and Kerremans (2012) studied the determinants of venue-shopping by interest groups. In so doing, they identified factors that facilitate and inhibit venue-shopping. These factors are primarily related to characteristics of the interest groups themselves and the issues at stake. By contrast, Damro's (2006) study of venue-shopping in international competition policy focuses on the characteristics of these international venues in order to explain why DG Competition has opted for some rather than others.

The other element in the theory, policy images and efforts at reframing them, have also received separate attention (Daviter 2009; Rhinard 2010). Taking the case of EU hedge fund regulation, Manuela Moschella (2011) has zoomed in on the limits of framing efforts. She argues that the framing of issues is strongly influenced both by the nature of the issue and by previous governance arrangements, which places clear limits on the extent to which actors can strategically reframe an issue.

All in all, then, 'earlier' PET has been applied to the EU by a wide range of scholars and in various policy areas. At the same time, the use of the terminology of PET – particularly the term 'venue-shopping' – does not automatically imply that PET is used. Several authors have used this term alongside or in combination with insights from other theories of the policy process, such as the advocacy coalition framework, Kingdon's (2003) multiple streams model, epistemic communities and institutionalist theories (e.g. Dudley and Richardson 1996; Mazey 1998; Parrish 2003; Radaelli 1999; Sabatier 1998). In this regard, 'venue-shopping' may go the same way as concepts such as Kingdon's (2003) 'window of opportunity', Haas's (1989) 'epistemic community' and Sabatier's (1998) 'advocacy coalitions', which are often used as convenient labels for describing widely observed phenomena, without using the underlying theories and the conditions they specify regarding the use of those terms.

3.2. Analysing change distributions in the EU

Whereas the case-study-oriented approach to PET, which analyses agenda-setting and policy change in terms of venue-image dynamics, has been widely applied to EU policy processes, applications of the approach that focuses on change distributions have been sparse. Moreover, analyses of change distribution on the basis of PET have been much more recent, with most research still in progress. One reason for this is the need for large-scale systematic databases to do the kind of statistical analysis that is required to study overall patterns of punctuated equilibrium. Analyses of punctuated equilibrium in an American context can build on datasets whose collection started in the early 1990s (Baumgartner *et al.* 1998). Attempts to build up such datasets for the EU have only occurred in the past few years, and existing analyses only yield tentative results. On the basis of these results, a number of preliminary conclusions can be drawn.

A first set of conclusions relates to the change pattern found in the EU. According to some studies, policy-making in the EU seems to conform to the pattern of punctuated equilibrium that has also been found in other political systems. Using datasets on the EU budget, both Baumgartner *et al.* (2007) and Citi (2013) found a punctuated change distribution. Baumgartner *et al.* (2007: 24) concluded that the EU is similar to national states in this regard. A similar result was obtained by Alexandrova *et al.* (2012) in their analysis of the issues discussed in European Council conclusions. Based on a dataset that codes over 40,000 (quasi-)sentences in all European Council conclusions between 1975 and 2010, they found a strongly punctuated change distribution. Focusing on a specific issue area (research and technology policy), Citi (2009) also observed a punctuated pattern of attention among EU policy-makers.

However, different outcomes are reported by a group of researchers at Sciences Po Paris, who have coded attention for issue in the EU's legislative acts (Dehousse *et al.* 2009). On the basis of preliminary data, they find that the pattern of change in the EU is much less punctuated than that found in the US (Grossman and Brouard 2009: 25–6). They suggest that this is so because the EU's legislative process is more isolated from public opinion than that in the US, both because popular politics plays a lesser role in EU politics and because the public spheres of the EU member states are less integrated.

As a result, the EU legislative agenda is not subject to the large swings in public opinion and the associated cascades that are important drivers of the US (and many other domestic) agendas.

It is difficult to assess the validity of these contradictory outcomes, since they look at different parts of the EU policy process and do not systematically compare the patterns found in the EU with those in other political systems. More systematic and refined analyses are therefore required before any firm conclusions can be drawn.

A second set of conclusions that can be drawn from existing quantitative work on the EU relates to the types of issues that receive most attention. Several studies show that the EU tends to have an atypical overall agenda, in which attention is strongly focused on a limited number of policy areas. For instance, compared to the US and France, the EU legislative agenda between 1999 and 2006 was dominated by macro-economic issues, agriculture and fisheries, employment and economic regulation (Grossman and Brouard 2009: 24). Together, these four policy areas accounted for 65 per cent of legislative acts. All other (16) policy areas that they discerned received little or no legislative attention. Using a similar coding scheme, Alexandrova *et al.* (2012: 75) found that almost 50 per cent of all (quasi-)sentences in European Council conclusions were devoted to just three policy areas: international affairs; macroeconomics; and governance issues. All other (18) policy areas lagged far behind.

Both studies suggest that EU agendas are relatively specialized. At the same time, they also show that there are large differences between agendas within the EU. After all, only one 'top' issue (macroeconomics) is shared between the two agendas in these studies. The other three policy areas that complete the top-four of the EU's legislative agenda, command much less attention in the European Council, while international affairs and governance issues are very important in the European Council but hardly lead to legislation. Here, too, a more fine-grained analysis that compares different EU agendas is necessary to obtain a clearer understanding of 'the' EU agenda and the roles played in it by the different EU institutions.

Comparing EU and US agendas, Princen (2009) studied the distribution of attention within two policy areas, health and environmental policy, showing both differences and similarities. Whereas the US health policy agenda was more or less equally divided between issues of public health (such as diseases, medicines and addictive substances) and healthcare (such as health insurance and the regulation of hospitals and health professionals), the EU agenda overwhelmingly focused on public health issues. In environmental policy, by contrast, the degree of similarity between the two systems was striking. Not only was the ranking of specific issues within this area more or less identical in the two systems, but differences in the relative attention given to issues were greater between the Commission and the EP than between the EP and US Congress. These results suggest that differences between the EU and US agendas are large where entire issue areas have been kept off the EU agenda (as is the case for healthcare issues), but that both systems produce much more similar agendas for issue areas that have gained a permanent position on the EU agenda (such as environmental policy).

A final set of studies focus on the interactions between agendas at the EU and member state levels. If we take seriously the claim that the EU is a multi-level polity in which policy-making involves (actors within) both the member states and the EU-level *per se*, any explanation of EU policy processes must take account of the interactions between and the processes taking place across these levels. A systematic study of policy agendas at both levels may contribute to such an understanding. Here, too, much work is still in its infancy, but scholars have started to use agendas data to study the impact of the EU on national policy-making (Brouard *et al.* 2012; Chaqués and Palau 2009), the role of EU issues in domestic elections (Green-Pedersen 2012), and the interaction of policy-making at the European and national levels (Princen *et al.* 2009).

4. CONCLUSIONS AND AGENDA FOR RESEARCH

Although the terminology of PET has become an established part of the EU policy-making literature, its use in the context of the EU has so far mainly been restricted to studies of venue-shopping. Although this has proven to be a valuable way of analysing and understanding EU policy dynamics, it has obscured the broader significance of the approach.

This broader significance of PET lies in how it approaches policy-making under conditions of high complexity and ambiguity. Both play crucial roles in explaining patterns of punctuated equilibrium and policy-making more generally. Complexity is a precondition for both venue-shopping and image shifts. For venue-shopping to take place, a political system needs to be characterized by the existence of multiple venues whose jurisdictions overlap. The complexity resulting from these multiple overlaps enables shifts of issues between venues. Likewise, image shifts are crucially dependent on the existence of multiple and overlapping aspects to the same issue. Because the complexity of issues is particularly taxing for human cognition and defies straightforward organizational formats, framing and re-framing are powerful ways of changing the prevailing perspective on an issue. This is further reinforced by the ambiguity inherent in many issue definitions, which allows for multiple competing and shifting images around one and the same issue.

In comparison with other approaches, the added value of PET lies in the way it integrates cognitive and institutional factors in one framework, under a unifying set of concepts and hypotheses. In so doing, it also brings together ideational and institutionalist accounts of policy-making as two sides of the same attentional processes.

These benefits are highly relevant in the context of the EU, with its multiple institutions, diverse membership and unclear institutional boundaries. More specifically, PET holds three promises for students of the EU. First, PET offers a way systematically to study the policy processes taking place within the EU, without resorting to idiosyncratic descriptions of the EU's institutional specificities. Second, PET, and its associated data collection methodology, allows for systematic comparisons between the EU and other polities, which is likely to promote our understanding of how the EU works compared to other political systems. Third, PET also offers an alternative way of analysing and understanding the longer-term process of European integration, by focusing on the dynamics of institutional and policy development in the EU (cf. Princen 2012).

For these promises of PET to be fulfilled, a more systematic use of the theory is needed, which moves beyond the mere notions of venue-shopping and framing and links them to the theory's underlying perspective on policy-making by individuals and organizations. A particularly fruitful avenue in this regard may be to combine large-scale quantitative datasets with a focus on specific issues as a way to link the two strands in the PET literature.

In doing so, three issues need to be addressed, which constitute an agenda for future research in this area. To begin with, the applicability and testability of PET in the context of the EU would be greatly enhanced by a clearer specification of the concept of policy change. The concepts of incremental and radical change imply that policy change is a one-dimensional concept, which ranges from 'small' to 'large'. In reality, policy change is often more complex, combining change in some parts of a policy programme with stasis in others. Moreover, policy instruments may change radically with a view to maintaining the overall objectives of a policy (Kay and Ackrill 2010). In these cases, it is difficult to apply a simple distinction between 'incremental' and 'radical' change, because the change process contains elements of both. For this reason, it is probably no coincidence that much of the (quantitative) applications of PET in domestic contexts have focused on budgetary outputs, which present unambiguous and one-dimensional measures of policy change. By contrast, change in regulatory policies is often much more ambiguous. Given the centrality of regulatory policies in EU politics, a more fine-grained methodology for assessing policy change is needed to enhance the applicability of PET, building on other work that has been done in the policy studies literature (Cashore and Howlett 2007; Hall 1993).

Second, studying patterns of policy change in the EU may contribute to our understanding of policy-making dynamics more generally. Recently, Michael Howlett and others have challenged the notion that punctuations and punctuated equilibria are the dominant pattern of policy change, pointing at policy domains in which fundamental policy change appears to have taken place without punctuations (Cashore and Howlett 2007; Howlett 2009). This raises the broader issue of the limits of PET. Is this a general theory of policy-making or does it describe a specific type of policy-making? If the latter is true, under what conditions is it applicable? Studying the EU can help move this debate forward because the EU differs from (democratic) domestic polities in a number of ways, most notably the high thresholds for making decisions and the smaller role of public opinion and 'popular politics'.

A third avenue for future research consists of attempts to synthesize attention- and preference-based explanations of policy-making. PET explains policy change by focusing on the allocation of attention and the processing of information. In so doing, it takes issue with approaches that take (change in) substantive preferences as their point of departure. This is a valuable addition, which has brought insights from the agenda-setting literature to the centre of the policy studies literature. Moreover, it is a particularly important addition to the EU studies literature, which has traditionally emphasized the importance of preferences and institutions for explaining policy outcomes, whether it is from a rational choice or a constructivist perspective. At the same time, PET's focus on attention has led it to neglect preferences as drivers of policy change. If one assumes, as seems reasonable, that policy change can be the result of either shifts in preferences or shifts in attention (or a combination of the two), then it is important to link these two change mechanisms and analyse the scope conditions under which each is relevant. This may lead to a fuller understanding of (EU) policy change, as well as a better understanding of the applicability and the limits of PET.

Biographical note: Sebastiaan Princen is Associate Professor at Utrecht University's School of Governance.

ACKNOWLEDGEMENTS

The author would like to thank Robert Ackrill, Marcello Carammia, Alasdair Young, Nikos Zahariadis and two anonymous referees for *JEPP* for their valuable comments on earlier versions of this article.

REFERENCES

Albaek, E., Green-Pedersen, C. and Nielsen, L.B. (2007) 'Making tobacco consumption a political issue in the United States and Denmark: the dynamics of issue expansion in comparative perspective', *Journal of Comparative Policy Analysis: Research and Practice* 9(1): 1–20.

Alexandrova, P., Carammia, M. and Timmermans, A. (2012) 'Policy punctuations and issue diversity on the European Council agenda', *Policy Studies Journal* 40(1): 69–88.

Baumgartner, F.R. *et al.* (2009) 'Punctuated equilibrium in comparative perspective', *American Journal of Political Science* 53(3): 603–20.

Baumgartner, F., Foucault, M. and François, A. (2007). 'Public budgeting in EU Commission: a test of the punctuated equilibrium thesis,' Communication presented at the *European Union Studies Association Conference*, Montreal, 17–19, May.

Baumgartner, F.R. and Jones, B.D. (1991) 'Agenda dynamics and policy subsystems', *The Journal of Politics* 53(4): 1044–74.

Baumgartner, F.R. and Jones, B.D. (1993) *Agendas and Instability in American Politics*, Chicago, IL, and London: University of Chicago Press.

Baumgartner, F.B., Jones, B.D. and MacLeod, M.C. (1998) 'Lessons from the trenches: ensuring quality, reliability, and usability in the creation of a new data source', *The Political Methodologist* 8(2): 1–10.

Beyers, J. and Kerremans, B. (2012) 'Domestic embeddedness and the dynamics of multilevel venue-shopping in four EU member states', *Governance* 25(2): 263–90.

Brouard, S., Costa, O. and König, T. (eds) (2012) *The Europeanization of Domestic Legislatures. The Empirical Implications of the Delors Myth in Nine Countries*, New York: Springer Verlag.

Cashore, B. and Howlett, M. (2007) 'Punctuating which equilibrium? Understanding thermostatic policy dynamics in Pacific Northwest forestry', *American Journal of Political Science* 51(3): 532–51.

Chaqués, L. and Palau, A. (2009) 'Comparing the dynamics of change in food safety and pharmaceutical policy in Spain', *Journal of Public Policy* 29(1): 103–26.

Citi, M. (2009) 'Patterns of policy evolution in the EU. The case of research and technology development policy', PhD dissertation, EUI, Florence, June 2009.

Citi, M. (2013) 'EU budgetary dynamics: incremental or punctuated-equilibrium?', *Journal of European Public Policy*, doi: 10.1080/13501763.2012.760333.

Cobb, R.W. and Elder, C.D. (1972) *Participation in American Politics. The Dynamics of Agenda-Building*, Baltimore, MD, and London: Johns Hopkins University Press.

Damro, C. (2006) 'The new trade politics and EU competition policy: shopping for convergence and co-operation', *Journal of European Public Policy* 13(6): 867–86.

Daviter, F. (2009) 'Schattschneider in Brussels: how policy conflict reshaped the biotechnology agenda in the European Union', *West European Politics* 32(6): 1118–39.

Dehousse, R., Deloche-Gaudez, F. and Jacquot, S. (eds) (2009) *Que Fait l'Europe?* Paris: Presses de Sciences Po.

Dudley, G. and Richardson, J. (1996) 'Why does policy change over time? Adversarial policy communities, alternative policy arenas, and British trunk roads policy 1945–95', *Journal of European Public Policy* 3(1): 63–83.

Fabbrini, S. (2003) 'A single Western state model? Differential development and constrained convergence of public authority organization in Europe and America', *Comparative Political Studies* 36(6): 653–78.

Green-Pedersen, C. (2007) 'The conflict of conflicts in comparative perspective: euthanasia as a political issue in Denmark, Belgium, and the Netherlands', *Comparative Politics* 39(3): 273–91.

Green-Pedersen, C. (2012) 'A giant fast asleep? Party incentives and the politicisation of European integration', *Political Studies* 60(1): 115–30.

Green-Pedersen, C. and Krogstrup, J. (2008) 'Immigration as a political issue in Denmark and Sweden', *European Journal of Political Research* 47(5): 610–34.

Green-Pedersen, C. and Wilkerson, J. (2006) 'How agenda-setting attributes shape politics: basic dilemmas, problem attention and health politics developments in Denmark and the US', *Journal of European Public Policy* 13(7): 1039–52.

Green-Pedersen, C. and Wolfe, M. (2009) 'The institutionalization of environmental attention in the United States and Denmark: multiple- versus single-venue systems', *Governance* 22(4): 625–46.

Grossmann, E. and Brouard, S. (2009) 'Quelles Sont les Priorités de l'Union Européenne?' in R. Dehousse, F. Deloche-Gaudez and S. Jacquot (eds) *Que Fait l'Europe?* Paris: Presses de Sciences Po, pp. 15–27.

Guiraudon, V. (2000) 'European integration and migration policy: vertical policy-making as venue shopping', *Journal of Common Market Studies* 38(2): 251–71.

Haas, P.M. (1989) 'Do regimes matter? Epistemic communities and Mediterranean pollution control', *International Organization* 43(3): 377–403.

Hall, P.A. (1993) 'Policy paradigms, social learning, and the state: the case of economic policymaking in Britain', *Comparative Politics* 25(3): 275–96.

Howlett, M. (2009) 'Process sequencing policy dynamics: beyond homeostasis and path dependency', *Journal of Public Policy* 29(3): 241–62.

Jensen, C. (2009) 'Policy punctuations in mature welfare states', *Journal of Public Policy* 29(3): 287–303.

John, P. and Margetts, H. (2003) 'Policy punctuations in the UK: fluctuations and equilibria in central government expenditure since 1951', *Public Administration* 81(3): 411–32.

Jones, B.D. and Baumgartner, F.R. (2005) *The Politics of Attention. How Government Prioritizes Problems*, Chicago, IL, and London: University of Chicago Press.

Jones, B.D., Sulkin, T. and Larsen, H.A. (2003) 'Policy punctuations in American political institutions', *American Political Science Review* 97(1): 151–69.

Kay, A. and Ackrill, R. (2010) 'Problems of composition, temporality and change in tracing the Common Agricultural Policy through time', *Journal of European Integration History* 16(2): 123–41.

Kingdon, J.W. (2003) *Agendas, Alternatives, and Public Policies*, 2nd edn, New York: HarperCollins College Publishers.

Mazey, S. (1998) 'The European Union and women's rights: from the Europeanization of national agendas to the nationalization of a European agenda?' *Journal of European Public Policy* 5(1): 131–52.

Mortensen, P.B. (2005) 'Policy punctuations in Danish local budgeting', *Public Administration* 83(4): 931–50.

Moschella, M. (2011) 'Getting hedge funds regulation into the EU agenda: the constraints of agenda dynamics', *Journal of European Integration*, 33(3): 251–66.

Parrish, R. (2003) 'The politics of sports regulation in the European Union', *Journal of European Public Policy* 10(2): 246–62.

Peters, B.G. (1994) 'Agenda-setting in the European Community', *Journal of European Public Policy* 1(1): 9–26.

Princen, S. (2009) *Agenda-Setting in the European Union*, Basingstoke: Palgrave.

Princen, S. (2010) 'Venue shifts and policy change in EU Fisheries Policy', *Marine Policy* 34(1): 36–41.

Princen, S. (2011) 'Agenda-setting strategies in EU policy processes', *Journal of European Public Policy* 18(7): 927–43.

Princen, S. (2012) 'Agenda-setting and the formation of an EU policy-making state', in J. Richardson (ed.), *Constructing a Policy-Making State? Policy Dynamics in the EU*, Oxford: Oxford University Press, 2012, pp. 29–45.

Princen, S. *et al.* (2009) 'Les Dynamiques d'Agendas Multiniveaux dans la Politique Environnementale de l'Union Européenne', *Revue Internationale de Politique Comparée* 16(3): 485–502.

Radaelli, C.M. (1999) 'The public policy of the European Union: whither politics of expertise?' *Journal of European Public Policy* 6(5): 757–74.

Rhinard, M. (2010) *Framing Europe: The Policy Shaping Strategies of the European Commission*, Dordrecht: Martinus Nijhoff.

Sabatier, P.A. (1998) 'The advocacy coalition framework: revisions and relevance for Europe', *Journal of European Public Policy* 5(1): 98–130.

Schattschneider, E.E. (1960) *The Semi-Sovereign People. A Realist's View of Democracy in America*, New York: Holt, Rinehart and Winston.

Sheingate, A.D. (2000) 'Agricultural retrenchment revisited: issue definition and venue change in the United States and European Union', *Governance* 13(3): 335–63.

True, J.L., Jones, B.D. and Baumgartner, F.R. (2007) '"Punctuated-equilibrium theory: explaining stability and change in public policymaking", in P.A. Sabatier (ed.), *Theories of the Policy Process*, Boulder, CO: Westview Press, pp. 155–87.

Walgrave, S. and Vliegenthart, R. (2010) 'Why are policy agendas punctuated? Friction and cascading in parliament and mass media in Belgium', *Journal of European Public Policy* 17(8): 1147–70.

Wendon, B. (1998) 'The Commission as image-venue entrepreneur in EU social policy', *Journal of European Public Policy* 5(2): 339–53.

Zahariadis, N. (2013) 'Building better theoretical frameworks of the European Union's policy process', *Journal of European Public Policy* 20(6), doi: 10.1080/13501763.2013.781815.

Ambiguity, multiple streams, and EU policy

Robert Ackrill, Adrian Kay and Nikolaos Zahariadis

ABSTRACT   The multiple streams framework draws insight from interactions between agency and institutions to explore the impact of context, time and meaning on policy change and to assess the institutional and issue complexities permeating the European Union (EU) policy process. The authors specify the assumptions and structure of the framework and review studies that have adapted it to reflect more fully EU decision-making processes. The nature of policy entrepreneurship and policy windows are assessed to identify areas of improvement. Finally, the authors sketch out a research agenda that refines the logic of political manipulation which permeates the lens and the institutional complexity which frames the EU policy process.

INTRODUCTION

The multiple streams framework (MSF) is a lens that was developed to explain United States (US) policy under conditions of ambiguity. It draws insight from interactions between agency and institutions to explain how the policy process works in 'organized anarchies', where there is a shifting roster of participants, opaque technologies and individuals with unclear preferences. Unlike previous reviews (Zahariadis 2007), we focus only on European Union (EU) adaptations to highlight the institutional and issue complexity of the EU context and the value-added from extending policy applications above the national level. What makes MSF particularly useful at the EU level is that it takes into account what are normally considered to be pathologies of the EU system, such as institutional fluidity, jurisdictional overlap, endemic political conflict, policy entrepreneurship and varying time cycles. We show how the lens's focus on context and agency productively explains the complex interactions among EU institutions, issues and policy entrepreneurs, but we also go beyond Zahariadis (2008) to stress the need for further clarification of testable hypotheses and the role of policy entrepreneurship.

The assumptions and structure of the framework are first specified. Applications in the EU context are then reviewed, outlining strengths and limitations. Finally, we chart a course for future research by pointing attention to valuable insight acquired by blending the MSF with neo-institutional approaches of EU policy.

ASSUMPTIONS AND STRUCTURE

In contrast to models of rational behaviour, the MSF accords significance to context and time – the latter being a scarce and valuable resource of policy-makers, whose primary concern is time, rather than task, management. Instead of choosing issues to solve, policy-makers are often forced to address a 'multitude of problems that are thrust upon them by factors beyond their control' (Kingdon 1995: 75). The MSF explores which issues get attention and when, how and which actors are mobilized to participate in a given choice opportunity, how issues are framed and meaning generated, and how the process is politically manipulated by skilled policy entrepreneurs. We use EU examples to illustrate the points made.

The lens makes three assumptions. First, *policy-makers operate under significant and varying time constraints.* In practice this means (a) they cannot attend to all problems, (b) they must use heuristics to get things done, and (c) they must accept outcomes that satisfice rather than optimize. Second, *means and ends, solutions and problems are generated independently of each other.* The implication is that information is vague, consequences are uncertain, and 'there appears to be no satisfactory way of determining an appropriate set of means or ends that would obtain sufficient agreement among a diverse set of stakeholders' (Alpaslan and Mitroff 2011: 23). Political conflict is endemic and issues are frequently settled by activating certain frames as EU actors move in and out of the process. Third, *ambiguity permeates the process.* Most actor preferences are opaque and not well defined; organizational technology is only partially comprehensible; participation is fluid. Information and institutions are not value-neutral. As a result, the process is open to political manipulation biased in favour of those who generate information, control access to policy venues, and synchronize or exploit group, national and institutional timetables.

MSF distinguishes between the world of organized anarchy and that of rationality. The MSF does not propose that individuals are acting in a manner inconsistent with their judgment of the best outcome. Adopting a system's point of view, it notes the system is not one of full information, clear goals and exact knowledge of the process. Indeed, policy-makers 'appear to be comfortable with an extraordinary array of [conflicting preferences and] unreconciled sources of legitimate wants' (March 1978: 599). In such a world no one controls the linkage between individual inputs and policy outputs; rather, ambiguity and randomness are part of normal EU policy-making and not pathologies that need to be rectified.

The lens contains five structural elements: *problems, policies, politics* (the three streams of the MSF); *windows of opportunity, and policy entrepreneurs.* The analytical task is to specify the dynamic and complex interactions that generate specific policy outcomes. Problems constitute conditions, measured by indicators often thrust into salience by focusing events (Birkland 1997), that policy-makers, interest groups and other policy actors believe warrant attention. Rapidly deteriorating public finances in Greece, bank implosions in Ireland and political conflict in Georgia are all problems that may warrant policy-maker attention. Policies are ideas or solutions that specialists develop to address pressing problems. Domestic fiscal reforms combined with external assistance to allow Greece to continue financing its sovereign debt and mediation in the Georgia conflict are solutions to problems of the day. Politics constitutes the broader environment within which policy is made. The ideological proclivity of incoming governments in EU capitals, the political muscle of bank lobbies in Brussels, and the partisan balance of power in the European Parliament constitute elements of the political stream.

Policy windows open in the politics or problem streams and describe the particular context within which issues are debated and policies made. They constitute triggers that delimit and/or help frame the way issues are debated. For example, the Madrid and London bombings in 2004 and 2005 ushered in new policies and a different attitude toward terrorism. Policy entrepreneurs are skilled and resourceful actors who couple the three streams together – problems, policies and politics – during open policy windows. Entrepreneurs are an important part of the process because policy is often not made in a rational, linear manner. In the presence of ambiguity of information and issue complexity, entrepreneurs craft contestable meaning, which they in turn disseminate to policy-makers in order to activate attention and mobilize support or opposition.

For example, the decision to bail out Greece involves far more than a cost–benefit analysis of Greek public finances. It is fundamentally a question of credibility, confidence, trust and faith – EU credibility in the eyes of investors and taxpayers, confidence in Greek ability to implement painful reforms, voter trust in German leadership, and faith in the euro. Moreover, to gain political traction a successful bailout depends vitally on framing reforms as promoting growth rather than imposing austerity. Entrepreneurs may be Commission officials by virtue of privileged position in EU information networks, prominent national policy-makers, high-level members of other EU institutions, or well-connected non-governmental organization (NGO) actors with a stake in EU policy.

Coupling is a major aspect of the MSF. Apart from skills and resources, entrepreneurs pursue strategies to join together problems and policies into attractive packages, which are then 'sold' to receptive policy-makers. The panoply of strategies includes appeals to higher-order national or EU symbols, framing as loss or gain, affect priming through mass arousal of public sentiment, and salami tactics. For example, as long as the problem remained framed as sinking Greek finances, EU policy-makers were collectively reluctant to assist Greece pay back its debt to private (ironically mostly EU) creditors. It was only after the risk of contagion threatened to engulf their own economies that aid 'to save the euro' became possible (Zahariadis 2012).

Taking the lens beyond the national level clearly demonstrates the need to specify how time cycles (Goetz 2009) also affect coupling. The short-term feedback from financial markets stands in stark contrast to long-term political calculations by national policy-makers. To take another example, the beginning of EU budget negotiations opens policy windows for a wide range of issues to be addressed. Paying attention to these negotiations depends partly on national electoral timetables, making co-ordination a crucial component of coupling. Policy entrepreneurs must straddle not only national but also EU institutional venues in ways that maintain domestic political support and still cultivate robustness of appeal to diverse audiences. The complexity of EU institutions serves as a valuable laboratory in which to test the conditions under which strategies of political manipulation work. The next section critically reviews those efforts.

A REVIEW OF APPLICATIONS IN THE EU CONTEXT

This section considers the uses to which the MSF has been put in academic writings. There is an extensive body of work which references Kingdon, frequently in the context of identifying individual elements of the MSF relevant as background to those papers (examples include the concept of the policy entrepreneur, windows of opportunity for policy-making, sometimes concepts as broad as agenda-setting), but without applying the ideas directly. A rather smaller number of articles draw on individual elements of the MSF in their own analyses. Fewer still apply what one might call the 'full' MSF to EU policy analysis.

In this section, we begin with a very brief overview of the origins of the MSF. After this, a small sample of papers is presented to illustrate how elements of the MSF have been utilized, but without the full model being called upon. This is followed by a fuller consideration of the key articles which have applied the MSF to EU issues. As we shall see, the first set of partial applications, which focus principally on agenda-setting, tend to come before the publication of Zahariadis (2003). The work of Zahariadis (notably Zahariadis 2003, 2008) marks a shift in the literature. By presenting arguments for two notable developments in the MSF, to analyse decision-making as well as agenda-setting; and to adapt the MSF to accommodate EU decision-making specificities, the foundation was laid for much of the empirical work which followed and which is explored below.

The starting point for the MSF, however, is Cohen *et al.* (1972). This analysis of 'organized anarchies' (universities, specifically) looked at organizational choice in the presence of problematic preferences, unclear technology and fluid participation. They argue (Cohen *et al.* 1972: 2) that 'one can view a choice opportunity as a garbage can into which various kinds of problems and policies are dumped by participants as they are generated.' They go on to say (*ibid.*: 2–3) that 'a decision is an outcome or interpretation of several relatively independent streams within an organization'. They identify four streams:

problems; solutions; participants; and choice opportunities. 'The garbage can process is one in which problems, solutions, and participants move from one choice opportunity to another' (*ibid.*: 16). Kingdon (1995: 86) follows the 'general logic' of Cohen *et al.*, but from his research into United States' federal health and transportation policies identifies three streams – problems, policies and politics.

In 2001, Johan Olsen identified the EU as 'an obvious candidate' for study using a garbage can approach (Olsen 2001: 196). He also stated that 'it may also be necessary to accept that significant political phenomena sometimes are complex enough to make any simpler theory of them unsatisfactory' (*ibid.*), which could be taken as a clarion call to which this collection, offering multiple approaches, is a response (see also Winn 1998).

Turning to some of the literature referencing the work of Kingdon, we begin with a sample of papers which highlight some of the constituent concepts used by academics, without their utilizing the full MSF. The implication of this is that these are concepts, embodied in the MSF, which are seen more widely as having particular relevance and importance in policy analysis. Examples include the (implicit) referencing of windows of opportunity and (policy) entrepreneurial activity (Cram 2001; see *inter alia* page 777). Policy entrepreneurs and entrepreneurship are also hinted at by Ringe (2005), in his analysis of the functioning of the European Parliament. His work also emphasizes both ambiguity and institutions (see also Corbett 2005: 153). Princen (2007), meanwhile, references Kingdon in the context of agenda-setting.

Early papers which utilize the MSF more fully in their analyses include, notably, Pollack (1997); Nugent and Saurugger (2002); Krause (2003); and Jordan *et al.* (2003). Krause (2003), and later, Corbett (2005), consider ambiguity as being a result of the institutional nature of the EU. Within that institutional structure, the Commission is often seen in these earlier contributions as a policy entrepreneur but, consistent with an agenda-setting view of the MSF, is not a part of the decision-making process. Nor is the Commission able to open a window of opportunity, but must wait for one to open.

One particular dimension of institutional structure in the EU which creates ambiguity is its multi-level nature (see also the contribution by Stephenson in this collection). Specifically, the Commission's role as policy entrepreneur:

> seems to depend largely on member state uncertainty regarding the problems and policies confronting them and on the Commission's acuity in identifying problems and policies that can rally the necessary consensus among member states in search of solutions to their policy problems. (Pollack 1997: 128; see also Jordan *et al.* 2003)

The role of the Commission as policy entrepreneur within the politics stream is an important part of the work of Nowak (2010). He compares two legal cases, Dassonville and Cassis de Dijon, through Kingdon's multiple streams lens. He identifies why, whilst these cases raised essentially the same legal issue in European Court of Justice rulings, the latter case resulted in the development of the policy concept of mutual recognition in intra-EU trade, a central concept in developing the Single European Market. Importantly, he distinguishes clearly what was lacking in the first case to prevent this policy development at that time.

The character of the window of opportunity also receives brief treatment. It has been argued that the opening of a window of opportunity, 'is not so much an active agent [of change] itself but rather a facilitator for the independent variables' (Nugent and Saurugger 2002: 349). These authors, drawing on Keeler (1993), also suggest that the wider the open window, the greater the possible change – with unpredictable events opening the window wider (an idea returned to below).

Turning to the more recent literature, Eberlein and Radaelli (2010) and Borrás and Radaelli (2011), along with Corbett (2005), are of particular interest, as they not only use the MSF but do so in conjunction with other analytical frameworks. Borrás and Radaelli embed (historical and discursive) institutionalism within the MSF (something Ackrill and Kay [2011] also do, albeit implicitly). Corbett explicitly draws on the work of Baumgartner and Jones (1993) to illuminate issue-definition and venue; and March (1994) to further the analysis of decision processes.

The aforementioned papers, however, typically adopt the MSF without adaptation to the specifics of EU policy processes. The nature and sources of ambiguity need to be defined clearly, partly as a result of which policy spillovers may not be of the type described by Kingdon (1995: 190–4), for whom a demonstration effect saw policy ideas copied in different policy arenas. Such institutional ambiguity may result in direct spillovers between linked policy arenas. Do these spillovers, in turn, affect the nature of the opening of a window?

The role of specific policy entrepreneurs needs careful delineation from the broader process of policy entrepreneurship (see, *inter alia*, Mintrom and Norman 2009; Ackrill and Kay 2011). Further, given the frequent identification in the extant literature of 'the Commission' (usually as a singular entity) as a policy entrepreneur, this challenges the idea of entrepreneurs being located outside of decision-making processes (although such an idea is consistent if the MSF is viewed solely as a means of analysing agenda-setting, but not decision-making).

Two papers which have gone furthest in trying to address these issues, are Natali (2004) and Ackrill and Kay (2011). Natali (2004: 1080) argues that policy entrepreneurs have the ability to help open windows, an idea that Corbett (2005) and, later, Ackrill and Kay (2011) develop. This is important given the position of the Commission within EU structures. The policy entrepreneur can, as Ackrill and Kay show, be an individual within the Commission. On the other hand, the sole right of the Commission to propose legislation puts the organization as a whole in a unique position regarding agenda-setting (although Peterson [1999] reports estimates that indicate, at that time, only between 10 and 25 per cent of all EU legislative proposals began life in the Commission).

Furthermore, as also explored by Ackrill and Kay (2011), the Commission is not a black box but an organization divided along thematic lines across which many policy issues span. This can itself be a source of ambiguity. These authors thus build on the earlier work of Nugent and Saurugger (2002: 351), who spoke of institutional ambiguity creating 'boundary problems', where policy issues overlap different policy arenas.

As for the nature of windows of opportunity, Nugent and Saurugger (2002) introduced the notion of windows being open a bit or a lot – which, in turn, influences the magnitude of the policy changes that are then possible. Natali (2004: 1079) also raises the width of the window as an issue. That said, his prime focus is on seeking to understand when a window will open. Specifically, 'variables do not float in the policy-making process, but combine with each other in a chain of events. A policy window is the result of an iterative process between problems, solutions, actors and events' Natali (2004: 1080). Ackrill and Kay (2011) took this idea in another direction, considering the length of time for which the window is open. Specifically, they consider situations where the window can be held open for a sustained period of time, thereby increasing the opportunities for decision-making to occur.

Such adaptations are not merely cosmetic, but have important implications for the MSF and its applicability to the study of EU policy processes. There is little disputing the fact that the EU, as an institutional structure, is highly complex and ambiguous (although in their analysis of the Lisbon Strategy, Borrás and Radaelli [2011] argue that, in policy areas relevant to the Strategy, the 2005 revision did go some way to clarifying the roles of Council and Commission).

A recent addition to the literature (Bache 2013), utilizes the MSF to look at an issue which, despite being very much part of policy discourse in recent years, has yet to receive policy attention. He analyses quality-of-life indicators as an input into public policy. Bache concludes that despite this idea receiving attention, it cannot yet be described as an idea whose time has come. Importantly, Bache identifies reasons why such measures have yet to yield policy responses. This is an important methodological contribution precisely because it improves our understanding of how the MSF can be applied to situations where there have not been policy responses to issues that, broadly speaking, have been identified as policy problems. Given the extent to which this issue has been attended to by politicians, it appears that a window of opportunity exists but which, for various technical and political reasons, has not resulted in a policy decision.

STRENGTHS AND LIMITATIONS

Strengths

While the MSF is valuable as a lens in organizing descriptions of EU policy-making processes, often unacknowledged is its contribution to meeting the challenge that confronts all temporally oriented policy studies: how to abstract from particular historical contexts and identify the extent to which regularities across historical time and space endure. A motivating force behind the MSF is the search for causal regularities in the policy process whilst, at the same time, allowing for the explanatory influence of contingency.

Although unexplored as yet in the EU policy process literature, there is potential for the MSF to be part of a fruitful dialogue with broader neo-institutionalist analysis in the study of EU policy-making. Notably, the MSF shares with institutionalism, especially the historical varieties, a stress on change being contingent on particular moments where the regular reproduction of patterns within institutionally complex environments is disrupted and reform moments present themselves. For example, the widely held view that institutions are always vulnerable and there is nothing automatic about stability, recently outlined and extended in Mahoney and Thelen (2010), chimes with the insights of the MSF into the critical moments which contain reform potential.

In recent accounts of institutional change, active coalitions are required to underpin institutional stability. There are moments when institutions are vulnerable to adaptation, conversion and exhaustion. Change comes from shifts in coalitions resulting from the interaction between institutions in complex environments and changes in the level and extent of institutional compliance. These change mechanisms have a family resemblance – albeit distant – to disturbances in the problem or policy streams that provide part of the causal driving force in explanations within the MSF. Furthermore, the proposition that institutions are always incomplete, often overlapping and ambiguous is commonplace in several 'new' institutionalisms. This requires a more refined attention to historical causality that goes beyond the excessively deterministic work in which actors appear to be institutional 'dopes' responding blindly to the requirements of the institution.

The MSF holds the possibility for the theoretical accommodation and perhaps extension of these approaches by providing elements to apprehend shifts in actor preferences from outside the institutionalized policy environment, as well as changes in actor strategies which can result in change at critical moments. The account of agency in the MSF is potentially rich; actors are rational but operate in particular contexts, and their rationality must be understood in such situational terms. Actors are self-determining and motivations may range from external regulation through to intrinsic regulation, which express themselves in creative policy-making strategies.

In Barzelay and Gallego (2006), the MSF is interpreted as allowing the analytical separation of the broader context from the analysis of particular situations. The MSF requires scholars to be simultaneously sensitive to how spillovers and focussing events may lead to fleeting moments in ongoing policy histories where reform potential exists, as well as understand the interaction between agents in such contexts at particular times. In such terms, the MSF is a mixture of the systemic and the situational and this is a major strength and novelty in the study of the EU policy process. Kingdon began the task of providing a set of causal mechanisms by which to explain contextual change in the US, as well as providing insights into whether policy change opportunities are actually exploited and a policy proposal enjoys a strong probability of being agreed and implemented. The challenge for EU policy scholars is to translate and adapt the MSF as appropriate to analysing the EU context.

As discussed, the coupling of separate sub-policy processes, and the role of the policy entrepreneurs therein, is the important causal driver in the MSF. The coincidence of three streams at certain moments greatly increases the likelihood that a policy reform is enacted. The framework places the policy entrepreneur in a context but, in stressing ideational effort and conscious political activity, it reveals that the context is not wholly exogenous to the model. The MSF specifies agency a function of institutionalized roles, but that specification is not so determined as to preclude creativity, and actors' strategies that are unexpected and influential in upsetting institutional scripts. Put another way, the openness and fluidity in the policy process is balanced by the recognition that explanations of sequences of policy-making can only be satisfying if they examine how the specific policy-making situation is bounded by a historically contingent context, including both formal and informal institutions.

Limitations

The limits of the MSF are in many respects consequent to its analytical novelty. It places the link between situations and broader context at the centre of understanding the EU policy process; yet the MSF remains limited in its ability so far to fully specify that link. The research agenda endures: how to understand policy entrepreneurs' situations in the broader context. Currently, much focus is on entrepreneurs as individuals with particular life experiences, aptitudes and policy preferences (see, for example, Corbett 2005). Such an analytical approach seemingly downplays the real ambition which girds the MSF: to illuminate the *ceteris paribus* clause for the comparative analysis of policy processes (Ackrill and Kay 2011). No entrepreneur alone will ever be enough to cause policy reform; we always require an account of the context. A *ceteris paribus* clause plays the role of fixing analytically the 'moment' replete with reform possibility. This facilitates claims such as 'this policy entrepreneurial strategy in this situation is successful only in this particular context'. If context changes in another case or over time – i.e., everything is not equal – then we cannot infer the same entrepreneurial causal mechanism will lead to reform. The expert and skilled advocacy of a policy idea, or skilled brokering, in one context does not produce reform; but exactly the same idea and brokering in a different context does produces reform. This is the causal structure behind the maxim that 'ideas have their time'.

There is an additional ideational mechanism connecting the three streams that is hinted at but not really developed in the MSF literature. The emergence of ideas within the policy stream may be considered analogous to natural selection: policy ideas circulate, combine and recombine in the garbage can but are selected by an environment of technical feasibility, value congruence, budgetary implications and political support. In this case, conditions of issue complexity can select certain proposals from within the policy stream; and policy change occurs in response to the nature of the policy window, as opposed to the advocacy or brokering entrepreneurial mechanisms where the policy window simply provides an opportunity for coupling. In this mechanism, the policy issue which is salient in the window may be of such complexity as to demand a unique solution or, at least, the number of policy solutions are so highly circumscribed that it is the nature of the window that does much of the explanatory heavy lifting, as opposed to entrepreneurial agency.

This variation in policy windows is an important challenge for future research using the MSF in the EU context. In particular, for the concept of windows of opportunity to provide analytical leverage within the MSF framework, it must escape the circular logic that all episodes of reform are windows of opportunity and that what characterizes a window of opportunity is evidence of policy change. The challenge for scholars is to distinguish, theoretically and empirically, non-change windows from those that result in change windows. Theoretical work on windows of opportunity where change or reforms do not eventuate is limited; as is sustained empirical analysis which recreates through counterfactual reasoning moments where reform possibility appears to exist but where no reforms are observed. Without a convincing account of failed opportunities, the MSF will be limited in both the range of policy processes it can account for as well as the explanatory power it can offer in the causal reconstruction of policy-making episodes.

As noted, coupling is the critical element in the MSF and is a function of both the nature of the policy window and the skills and resources of the policy entrepreneur. However, almost all the literature focuses on the latter element rather than the first. In the original Kingdon model, the streams are independent, and thus the opening of a window in either the politics or problem streams is not causally related to the policy stream. Instead, the policy stream is a transmission belt of previous policy decisions, policy analyses and the nature of the policy discourse. Within the stream there are networks of policy entrepreneurs who mediate the emergence of policy ideas and attempt to increase the receptivity of policy-makers to their ideas.

Importantly, what emerges as a potential solution in response to the opening of a policy window is the result of prior advocacy for ideas and proposals by entrepreneurs, in particular their skill, persistence and resources in pushing particular project. For MSF applications to the EU, it is their ability to sell these ideas to policy makers in response to policy windows – and thereby couple the politics, problems and policy streams – that explains whether windows of policy opportunity actually result in policy change.

However, this account of coupling fails to capture the intuition in broader policy scholarship of a mood of 'something needing to be done'. In a manner consistent with MSF insights into situations where policy solutions exist in search of a problem or rationale, there is the logical possibility that agendas may be used by policy-makers to search out proposals. When these windows occur in the political stream, the agenda may be short term or symbolic, forcing a search for politically successful policies. These are not obviously related to solving policy problems and the MSF contains no presumption of rationality in the policy process. Policy may be decided by the coupling of the politics and policy streams, which subsequently drives a search for elements in the problem stream that might serve to legitimize the already-decided policy.

In the case of windows creating short-term, time-pressured political agendas which act as filter mechanisms for ideas in the policy stream, the role for policy entrepreneurs becomes limited. They still advocate and keep ideas available for selection by policy-makers driven by short-term political pressures, but their brokerage role is bounded in explaining when, why and in what form policy change is enacted. Instead, it is the nature of the policy window and the reform agenda it creates for policy-makers which plays the primary causal role in shaping which policy ideas gain attention.

This, however, leads back us back to the limits of the MSF. For example, Corbett (2005) locates policy entrepreneurs in the higher levels of the Commission. This is perfectly reasonable for the study of EU policy processes, but in doing so the distinction between policy entrepreneurs and policy-makers in the politics stream becomes blurred. Furthermore, for Corbett it is essential to appreciate that these are *individuals* with life histories, personal beliefs, identities as well as an institutional position. Thus, you must understand them, beyond just their institutional context, to apprehend fully their influence in policy change.

This is indubitably true, but it leaves us with a research agenda about policy entrepreneurship: why do some succeed and others fail in different contexts? Why are some able to discern and exploit opportunities and others not? To the extent that the effectiveness of policy entrepreneurs is a function of institutional position, what does the concept add? Does the term mean anything without analysis of the particular situation in which opportunities occur (i.e., entrepreneurship *qua* actions can only be judged in a particular situation)?

There is a further alternative mechanism that focuses on a policy window in either the politics or problem stream forcing or enabling policy-makers to search for solutions. Instead of passive agents who are sold coupling strategies by policy entrepreneurs, or bound by issue complexity to a highly circumscribed set of policy options, they employ intentional selection mechanisms to select a policy solution that is appropriate for the nature of the agenda set by the policy window. Thus, policy solutions can make it onto the decision agenda not because they are sold by the persistence and skill of policy entrepreneurs but rather because policy-makers select the ideas (as appropriate for the policy window) and thus the policy entrepreneurs who advocate. This alternative specification further limits in the concept of policy entrepreneurship: most pertinently, are those whom we have hitherto called policy-makers actually policy entrepreneurs?

In the MSF literature, the answer is ambiguous. For some, policy entrepreneurs sit outside the formal decision-making process. However, as noted above, subsequent scholarship (particularly in applications to the EU) has also placed policy entrepreneurs in senior bureaucratic positions. If policy entrepreneurs can be in high formal office as well as outside the formal machinery of policy-making, then the policy entrepreneurship concept is stretched. Doing so conflates two separate mechanisms in policy-making: the *selling* of ideas to policy-makers and the *selecting* of ideas by policy-makers. Both may be entrepreneurial. One suggestion is to understand entrepreneurship as a general label for a set of behaviours in the policy process, rather than a permanent characteristic of an individual or a particular role. On this argument, entrepreneurs can be from anywhere and the challenge is to distinguish those policy-makers who play their institutional role from those who qualify as entrepreneurs in particular reform episodes. The attribution of causality to agency *qua* policy entrepreneurship is only ever temporary and acutely sensitive to the particular context and situation.

The discussion of entrepreneurship in EU policy-making tends to rely on the unstated argument that entrepreneurial characteristics at the individual level are not normally distributed in the population; there is something distinctive about the individuals who are policy entrepreneurs. However, this attribution is always done *ex post* and always to political actors involved in actual reform. Our understanding of policy entrepreneurship thus becomes significantly limited. For instance, we have no analytical means of explaining successful entrepreneurship because we have no sample of failed entrepreneurial strategies. Perhaps more importantly, we equate successful entrepreneurship with actual reform, but what about agency in defence of the *status quo*? There are various strategies employed by actors to preserve institutions and policy systems against reform strategies. Therefore, we can only really explain entrepreneurship in terms of actions in a particular context. This is perhaps better expressed as policy entrepreneurship not being a stable characteristic that differentiates policy agents in all situations; but rather as referring to actions in certain policy-making situations.

The implication of placing EU issue and institutional complexity at the heart of the development of frameworks for the analysis of the EU policy process is that any framework or lens, individually, will be incomplete. The acknowledgement of complexity as the central feature of life in the EU undermines any search for a general theory of EU policy-making. Pluralism rather than monism underpins the intellectual project of this collection. The MSF contributes much to this endeavour in its ability to complement other approaches, most particularly those which provide accounts of the causal logic of institutional variables. The MSF analysis privileges links between the broader contextual regularities and patterns, and situational moments of contingency where policy-making processes may end up heading in unexpected and unpredictable directions. The three streams, their coupling, and the role of agency therein provide analytical leverage on periods of relative policy stability as well as specific moments where things are open to change.

As it stands, the MSF is not formally articulated as a theory or model that might allow empirical testing of its predictive accuracy. Indeed, it is moot whether this is a desirable ambition for a framework whose strongest empirical achievements to date have been to offer temporally oriented perspectives on EU policy. It may be more productive to develop the MSF in conjunction with other EU policy process approaches explored here, rather than as a competitor. This kind of pluralism suggests that although different lenses might be rivalrous in the analysis of any particular reform episode, under similar conditions they may be additive rather in terms of overall explanatory power available for apprehending highly specific combinations of causal mechanisms across time and different EU policy sectors. Pragmatist philosopher C.S. Pierce argues that different frameworks should be viewed as strands braided together into a rope, instead of links in a chain. With links in a chain, if there is even one weak link it does not matter whether different approaches are competitive or complementary in any particular instance. However, while individual strands in a rope may not be strong enough to support the explanatory weight for which they are needed, they may be stronger when braided together.

WHERE DO WE GO FROM HERE?

The MSF has proven useful in identifying and helping to resolve puzzles of EU policy processes and policy-making. Its usefulness lies in the lens's capacity to handle ambiguity and its ability to capture the complex interactions among institutions, issues and entrepreneurs. This has particular resonance in the EU case, with its unique and highly complex multi-level decision-making process. However, as we argued above, the MSF's novelty is also its limitation. The focus on context and agency is an important but analytically difficult enterprise because it demands access to significant amounts of information to explain without the promise of corresponding ability to predict. To be sure, MSF incorporates randomness into the explanation so it cannot predict which individual events or outcomes will occur. But it can generate expectations that increase the likelihood of some outcomes occurring and not others. Clarifying causal drivers and specifying testable hypotheses will go a long way toward augmenting explanatory power and enhancing our understanding of probabilistic expectations.

Research clarifying the lens's internal causal drivers and hypotheses, undertaken in recent papers through reflection on the MSF in the EU context, offers considerable promise for future research. Recent work has begun to enhance our understanding of both agenda-setting and decision-making; of the distinction between policy entrepreneurs as individuals and policy entrepreneurship as a process; of 'boundary problems' – policy spillovers potentially being endogenous as well as exogenous – and of the implications of that distinction for policy-making; and of policy entrepreneurs participating in decision-making and opening policy windows. These developments are important because they give the MSF greater nuance and sophistication.

We do not argue that a singular, universal, multiple streams lens can be developed for use in all EU circumstances; adaptation of the lens may be required. But this is an essential feature of the MSF and why it is so well-suited to applications where agenda-setting and decision-making are replete with ambiguities. Clarification of the lens's internal causal drivers and their adaptation to the EU context hold considerable promise for future research. For example, the EU's institutional context and varying timescapes are uniquely suited to further specification of coupling as an institutional venue-shopping strategy. Under what conditions do hierarchical versus non-hierarchical institutional arrangements promote venue-shopping and success? How do policy windows influence the 'shopping' process? Links with the literature on punctuated equilibria (Princen 2013) and multi-level governance (Stephenson 2013) may provide fruitful collaborative research in these areas. Given the proclivity of EU mechanisms for co-operation and for limiting conflict, how do frame contests work across issues? Daviter (2011) provides some examples from the biotechnology field, but more work needs to be done to capture fully the conditions of entrepreneurial success and its interaction with broader political forces, including the presence or absence of a 'European' mood, which is a concept that features prominently in national applications of the MSF (e.g., Kingdon 1995).

Another feature of the MSF lens which makes it suitable to application to the EU context is its fluidity. The three streams not only ebb and flow in relation to each other but, in so doing, transverse and connect different levels of policy actors. EU policy-making processes are relatively stable, but actor participation in policy-making is fluid and the policy issues considered at the EU level is growing. The deliberately loose coupling between means and ends, choice and implementation, what Héritier (1999) calls the strategy of subterfuge, has served member states well so far. However, an expansion of EU policy competences increasingly implies member states are giving up sole jurisdiction over a range of policy issues. At the same time, there continue to be debates over the extent to which the EU suffers from a democratic deficit (e.g., Crombez 2003; Moravcsik 2002).

The MSF predicts political conflict will rise, increasing the importance of policy entrepreneurs and their strategies. At the same time, democratic accountability through representation remains unchanged even if some cosmetic changes are made, such as the proposal to elect the President of the Commission through popular elections. A major task for the MSF is to specify channels of democratic accountability in light of increasing complexity and political acrimony. Does greater EU institutional complexity actually increase democratic accountability and transparency, or does the presence of more institutional venues give rise to more opportunities for political manipulation and lower transparency?

Institutional and issue complexity amplify dramatically through jurisdictional overlap, while accountability is diffused among multiple institutions and actors. One may view such developments as increasing the potential number of policy windows available for entrepreneurs to push through pet proposals that apply throughout the EU, but for which groups of voters have little input. Assuming the distribution of timescapes does not change dramatically, the likelihood of such opportunities will multiply, intensifying political manipulation struggles. As Krause (2003) implies in his study of the Common Foreign and Security Policy (CFSP), there are, quite simply, an expanding number of areas of EU activity to which the MSF can be applied. Any takers?

Biographical notes: Robert Ackrill is Professor of European Economics and Policy at Nottingham Business School, UK. Adrian Kay is an Associate Professor in the Crawford School of Economics and Government at the Australian National University, Canberra. Nikolaos Zahariadis is Professor and Director of Political Science at the Department of Government, University of Alabama at Birmingham, USA.

ACKNOWLEDGEMENT

We wish to thank the *JEPP* referees for their helpful comments on earlier drafts. We also wish to thank all participants at the workshop held at the University of Alabama at Birmingham, 9–10 March 2012 for their extremely helpful comments. The usual disclaimer applies.

REFERENCES

Ackrill, R. and Kay, A. (2011) 'Multiple streams in EU policy-making: the case of the 2005 sugar reform', *Journal of European Public Policy* 18(1): 72–89.
Alpaslan, C.M. and Mitroff, I.I. (2011) *Swans, Swine, and Swindlers*, Stanford, CA: Stanford University Press.
Bache, I. (2013) 'Measuring quality of life for public policy: an idea whose time has come? Agenda-setting dynamics in the European Union', *Journal of European Public Policy* 20(1): 21–38.
Barzelay, M. and Gallego, R. (2006) 'From "new institutionalism" to "institutional processualism": advancing knowledge about public management policy change', *Governance* 19(4): 531–57.
Baumgartner, F. and Jones, B. (1993) *Agendas and Instability in American Politics*, Chicago, IL: University of Chicago Press.
Birkland, T.A. (1997) *After Disaster: Agenda-Setting, Public Policy and Focusing Events*, Washington, DC: Georgetown University Press.

Borrás, S. and Radaelli, C.M. (2011) 'The politics of governance architecture: creation, change and effects of the EU Lisbon Strategy', *Journal of European Public Policy* 18(4): 463–84.

Cohen, M.D., March, J.G. and Olsen, J.P. (1972) 'A garbage can model of organizational choice', *Administrative Science Quarterly* 17: 1–25.

Corbett, A. (2005) *Universities and the Europe of Knowledge: Ideas, Institutions and Policy Entrepreneurship in European Union Higher Education Policy, 1955-2005*, Basingstoke: Palgrave Macmillan.

Cram, L. (2001) 'Whither the Commission? Reform, renewal and the issue-attention cycle', *Journal of European Public Policy* 8(5): 770–86.

Crombez, C. (2003) 'The democratic deficit in the European Union: much ado about nothing?' *European Union Politics* 4(1): 101–20.

Daviter, F. (2011) *Policy-Framing in the European Union*, Basingstoke: Palgrave Macmillan.

Eberlein, B. and Radaelli, C.M. (2010) 'Mechanisms of conflict management in EU regulatory policy', *Public Administration* 88(3): 782–99.

Goetz, K.H. (2009) 'How does the EU tick? Five propositions on political time', *Journal of European Public Policy* 16(2): 202–20.

Héritier, A. (1999) *Policy-Making and Diversity in Europe*, Cambridge: Cambridge University Press.

Jordan, A., Wurzel, R., Zito, A.R. and Brückner, L. (2003) 'European governance and the transfer of "new" environmental policy instruments (NEPIs) in the European Union', *Public Administration* 81(3): 555–74.

Keeler, J. (1993) 'Opening the window for reform', *Comparative Political Studies* 25(4): 433–86.

Krause, A. (2003) 'The European Union's Africa policy: the Commission as policy entrepreneur in the CFSP', *European Foreign Affairs Review* 8: 221–37.

Kingdon, J. (1995) *Agendas, Alternatives and Public Policies*, 2nd edn, New York: Harper Collins.

Mahoney, J. and Thelen, K. (eds) (2010) *Explaining Institutional Change: Ambiguity, Agency, and Power*, Cambridge: Cambridge University Press.

March, J. (1978) 'Bounded rationality, ambiguity and the engineering of choice', *Bell Journal of Economics* 9: 587–608.

March, J. (1994) *A Primer on Decision-Making*, New York: Free Press.

Mintrom, M. and Norman, P. (2009) 'Policy entrepreneurship and policy change', *Policy Studies Journal* 37(4): 649–67.

Moravcsik, A. (2002) 'In defence of the "democratic deficit": reassessing legitimacy in the European Union', *Journal of Common Market Studies* 40(4): 603–24.

Natali, D. (2004) 'Europeanization, policy arenas, and creative opportunism: the politics of welfare state reforms in Italy', *Journal of European Public Policy* 11(6): 1077–95.

Nowak, T. (2010) 'Of garbage cans and rulings: judgements of the European Court of Justice in the EU legislative process', *West European Politics* 33(4): 753–69.

Nugent, N. and Saurugger, S. (2002) 'Organizational structuring: the case of the European Commission and its external policy responsibilities', *Journal of European Public Policy* 9(3): 345–64.

Olsen, J.P. (2001) 'Garbage cans, new institutionalism, and the study of politics', *American Political Science Review* 95(1): 191–8.

Peterson, J. (1999) 'The Santer era: the European Commission in normative, historical and theoretical perspective', *Journal of European Public Policy* 6(1): 46–65.

Pollack, M.A. (1997) 'Delegation, agency, and agenda setting in the European Community', *International Organization* 51(1): 99–134.

Princen, S. (2007) 'Agenda-setting in the European Union: a theoretical exploration and agenda for research', *Journal of European Public Policy* 14(1): 21–38.

Princen, S. (2013) 'Punctuated equilibrium theory and the European Union', *Journal of European Public Policy* 20(6), doi: 10.1080/13501763.2013.781822.

Ringe, N. (2005) 'Policy preference formation in legislative politics: structures, actors, and focal points', *American Journal of Political Science* 49(4): 731–45.

Stephenson, P. (2013) 'Twenty years of multi-level governance: "Where Does It Come From? What Is It? Where Is It Going?"', *Journal of European Public Policy* 20(6), doi: 10.1080/13501763.2013.781818.

Winn, N. (1998) 'Who gets what, when, and how? The contest conceptual and disciplinary nature of governance and policy-making in the European Union', *Politics* 18(2): 119–32.

Zahariadis, N. (2003) *Ambiguity and Choice in Public Policy: Political Manipulation in Democratic Societies*, Washington, DC: Georgetown University Press.

Zahariadis, N. (2007) "The multiple streams framework: structure, limitations, prospects", in P.A. Sabatier (ed.), *Theories of the Policy Process*, 2nd edn, Boulder, CO: Westview Press, pp. 65–92.

Zahariadis, N. (2008) 'Ambiguity and choice in European public policy', *Journal of European Public Policy* 15(4): 514–30.

Zahariadis, N. (2012) 'Complexity, coupling, and policy effectiveness: the European response to the Greek sovereign debt crisis', *Journal of Public Policy* 32(2): 99–116.

Constructivism and public policy approaches in the EU: from ideas to power games

Sabine Saurugger

ABSTRACT   The aim of this contribution is to critically analyse the strengths and pitfalls of constructivist public policy approaches in European Union (EU) studies and to develop avenues for further research. Four conceptual frameworks are more specifically discussed: (1) sociological institutionalism; (2) discursive institutionalism; (3) approaches based on socialization and learning;, and finally (4) actor-centred constructivism. When the constructivist turn in international relations 'hit' European integration theories, the large epistemological tent under which constructivists gathered centred schematically around two puzzles: how ideas, norms and world views were established; and how and why they mattered. Recently, actor strategies and economic rationality have been reintroduced into constructivist accounts. This actor-centred constructivism is very much based on the idea that in order to understand how actors think and how their ideas count in policy-making, one must take into account the way actors use ideas strategically. This contribution argues that this perspective allows us to reach beyond the dichotomy opposing rational choice and more interpretative approaches and helps us to best understand how ideas influence policy processes.

INTRODUCTION

Constructivist approaches have mushroomed since the 1990s in theoretical accounts of various areas of European integration (Christiansen *et al.* 1999; Eilstrup-Sangiovanni 2006; Rosamond 2000; Risse 2004, 2009; Surel 2000). In the field of public policy these approaches focus on the social construction of policy problems or frames of reference on which policy-making is based. The main question is how ideational factors (worldviews, ideas, collective understandings, norms, values, cognitive schemes, etc.)[1] dominate political action (Abdelal *et al.* 2010; Berman 1998; Blyth 1997, 2002; Checkel 1993; Cox 2001; Culpepper 2008; Fischer 2003; Genyies and Smyrl 2008; Gofas and Hay 2010; Goldstein and Keohane 1993; Hall 1993; McNamara 1998; Parsons 2002, 2010; Schmidt and Radaelli 2004; Wendt 1999).

However, the widespread use of the term 'constructivist turn' or 'ideational turn' in public policy gives the impression there is a coherent conceptual framework. This is not the case. Constructivist accounts have taken various forms and can be understood from different vantage points reaching from post-positivist constructivists, who explore the discursive practices that make certain norms in the European Union (EU) possible in the first place (Checkel 2006; Diez 1999), to 'conventional' constructivists, whose aim is to analyse how ideational factors influence policy outcomes (Béland and Cox 2011; Genyies and Smyrl 2008; Gofas and Hay 2010). My purpose is not to propagate an overarching theory of constructivism in European public policy. Rather, I seek to map common ground as well as differences among scholars engaged in the four constructivist public policy perspectives that can be found in EU studies: (1) sociological institutionalism; (2) discursive institutionalism; (3) approaches based on socialization and learning; and finally (4) actor-centred constructivism. Consistent with the overall aim of this collection, the objective here is to explore the extent to which these perspectives help us to better understand the ambiguity and complexity of policy-making processes in the EU. Discussing them in turn is crucial in order to give the flavour of diversity that exists, but also to highlight the progression of constructivist thinking in these areas. While each sociological and discursive institutionalism did not necessarily develop in direct competition to the other, each evolved in ways that sought to address some of the limitations of others. The categories built in this contribution are not airtight; rather, their boundaries are contested, as are the main concepts around which they revolve.

This contribution argues that interest in ideational aspects of policy-making processes make constructivist approaches particularly useful at explaining policy outcomes in a context of high issue complexity. While in policy processes in general actors often have not a clear and well-articulated set of preferences (Zahariadis 1999, 2003) or, better, have contradictory preferences which are embedded in specific values and worldviews, this situation is even more acute at the European level where the amount and the nature of informal linkages, as issue complexity is defined in this collection, is very high (Zahariadis 2013). The result is an uneven integration in the EU across issues based on different worldviews and a large number of diverse rules. It is the influence of these worldviews on policy-making processes that constructivist public policy perspectives are able to better explain.

The first three constructivist perspectives analysed in this contribution – sociological and discursive institutionalism, and approaches based on socialization and learning – either explicitly or implicitly insist on the clear difference between rationalist and constructivist thinking. They reject the assumption that material factors are the main independent variable, as rational choice scholars claim (Mueller 2003), and argue that ideational factors frame the understanding of these material factors (for an in-depth debate of this 'intellectual topography of ideational explanations', see Gofas and Hay [2010: 3]). These ideational factors shed light on the influence of 'world views', mechanisms of identity formation, and principles of action in public policy analysis. The fourth perspective – actor-centred constructivism – attempts to transcend this dichotomy (Blyth 2002; Hall 1993; Jabko 2006; McNamara 1998; Parsons 2002; Surel 2000) and helps us not to underestimate the forms of mobilization to which these factors are subject.

Indeed, the idea of the strategic behaviour of actors has found its way back into constructivist approaches centred on public policy. The assumption of this 'actor-centred' constructivism is to understand how worldviews, which provide the cognitive background in which actors evolve, are at the same time used by actors to strategically achieve their goals. In this perspective, ideas and norms do not solely constitute the environment in which actors are embedded (constitutive logic), but are also tools consciously used by these same actors to attain their goals (causal logic). This allows us not to obscure the fact that power is unequally distributed amongst actors. At the same time, this branch of constructivism is no longer exclusively centred on cognitive factors as opposed to materialistic factors: both must be taken into account (Gofas and Hay 2010). My argument here is consistent with this idea: only approaches that succeed in combining both logics, a constitutive and a causal one, provide the necessary tools to understand policy processes in the European Union.

In line with the aims of this collection, the contribution attempts to be both a critique of constructivist approaches to public policy in EU studies and provide avenues that might help us to combine rationalist and idealist logics. It does so in three parts: a first part will present the main questions that constructivist approaches address in the field of public policy research in general; a second part will then more precisely present the specific issues and concerns in particular approaches to EU policy studies; before presenting in a third and last part an agenda for future research.

CONSTRUCTIVISM IN PUBLIC POLICY ANALYSIS

On the most general level, constructivism refers to the assumption that social norms and frameworks on which reality is based are constructed and redefined through permanent interaction (Berger and Luckmann 1966). Actors' interests cannot be understood as deduced from a solely material structure, as rational choice approaches would argue (Elster 1989; Mueller 2003). Rational choice derives preferences exogenously by specifying properties (position, resources, etc.) across actors and how different values of properties imply different preferences. On the contrary, constructivists assume that social, political and economic contexts structure these interests; thus, actors and structures are co-constituted – one of the most central terms in constructivist research. In other words, the way we think about the world makes the world as we perceive it. Thus, constructivists have a very different understanding of how interests change. For materialists, actors' interests evolve as changes in their environment alter their situation. Constructivists, or idealists, on the contrary, assume that interests change as agents alter their understanding of their changing world and recalculate their priorities (Béland and Cox 2011).

The importance of this co-constitution of agents and structures is reflected by the opposition of two logics: a logic of appropriateness; and a logic of consequentialism (in particular March and Olsen [1998]; for a less constructivist and more sociological perspective, see March and Olsen 1984, 1989). Whereas the logic of consequentialism treats agents and structures as two distinct features that explain political processes (the goal of action is to maximize one's own interests and preferences), the logic of appropriateness allows for the conceptualizing of this co-constitution of actors and structures. The logic of appropriateness is:

> a perspective that sees human action as driven by rules of appropriate or exemplary behaviour, organized into institutions. Rules are followed because they are seen as natural, rightful, expected, and legitimate. Actors seek to fulfil the obligations encapsulated in a role, an identity, a membership in a political community or group, and the ethos, practices and expectations of its institutions. (March and Olsen 2004: 2)

Thus, acting according to a logic of appropriateness is more a question of behaving correctly in policy-making processes, in line with criteria established by a society or a group, than maximizing one's preferences (Ostrom 1999).

The logic of appropriateness refers to ideas (Béland 2009), or, in other words to the 'collective understandings of social facts', as the primary source of political behaviour. These 'claims about descriptions of the world, causal relationships, or the normative legitimacy of certain actions' (Parsons 2002: 48), influence policy development in three ways (Béland 2009: 702). First, they help to construct the problems and issues that enter the policy agenda; second, they frame the basic assumptions that influence the content of reform proposals; finally, ideas can act as discursive tools that shape reform imperatives.

To what extent does this help us to better understand, on the one hand, issue complexity, and on the other, the ambiguity of EU public policy making? Not paying attention to the embeddedness of actors in cognitive frames may obfuscate major aspects of policy-making. Not only is it important that policy decision and policy reforms have been taken, but also why the agents of policy processes sometimes do not react as expected. Their rationality is embedded in specific cognitive frames that must be understood in order to make sense of, sometimes, ambiguous behaviour.

SPECIFIC ISSUES AND CONCERNS IN CONSTRUCTIVIST APPROACHES TO EU PUBLIC POLICY

Based on these general elements, constructivists analysing EU public policies have developed four conceptual perspectives, each of which concentrates on specific aspects of policy making. Two are more specifically linked to institutionalist approaches, and two deeply anchored in social constructivism and

Table 1 Constructivist approaches to public policy

	Sociological institutionalism	*Socialization and Learning*	*Discursive institutionalism*	*Actor-centred constructivism*
Elements explaining change	Informal institutions, identity, shared experiences, cognitive frameworks	Formal and informal institutions	Informal institutions, discourses and ideas	Formal and informal institutions, rational calculation.
Subject of analysis	Cultural standards and cognitive frameworks	Actors' attitudes in decision-making processes	Ideas and discourses	Rational calculation framed by embeddedness in formal and informal institutions
Logic of explanation	Logic of social conventions	Socialization and learning	Communication	Strategic calculation

sociology: (1) sociological institutionalism; (2) socialization and learning; (3) discursive institutionalism; and (4) actor-centred constructivism. The last approach is rooted in one of the central critiques of constructivist approaches – i.e., the absence of considerations about authority and power. This last approach has become one of the most promising conceptual frameworks in EU public policy research, as it allows for the considering of both the strategic interests of actors as well as their embeddedness in cognitive structures. Thus, actor-centred constructivism goes beyond the opposition between agent behaviour based on a logic of consequentialism and that based on a logic of appropriateness. Both logics co-exist and influence the attitudes of actors in policy-making processes.

Table 1 summarizes the four constructivist accounts of EU public policy approaches, through three specific features that will be explained in more detail in the remaining specific sub-sections of this contribution: elements explaining change; the subject of analysis; and the logic of explanation.

Sociological institutionalism

In both institutionalist approaches to constructivist public policy concepts, institutions are understood as rules, norms and strategies (Ostrom 1999: 37). Sociological institutionalism is not a constructivist perspective as such but contains elements constructivists have used extensively, and thus makes it necessary to include it in this debate. In a certain sense, it seems to be a source on which constructivists in EU public policy have built the three other constructivist perspectives. It more specifically derives from the different conceptualizations of organizational sociology and puts particular emphasis on the cognitive dimensions of institutional actions. These cognitive dimensions can be understood through four attitudes in particular: logic of appropriateness; logic of consequentialism; isomorphism; and mimesis (Peters 2005). The two logics have been discussed above and, as we have seen, have tremendously influenced debate in public policy studies in general.

The third element, isomorphism, results from social processes of emulation and diffusion. Sociological institutionalism argues that in policy-making processes actors replicate organizational models collectively sanctioned as appropriate and legitimate (Dimaggio and Powell 1991; March and Olsen 1984, 1989). Three mechanisms of institutional isomorphic change can be identified: coercion; mimesis; and normative pressures. Coercive isomorphism refers to pressure from other organizations, mostly the government, via public subsidies, upon which institutions are dependent. Coercive isomorphism can also be exercised by cultural expectations stemming from society as institutions conforming to expectations from the outside. In EU studies, the main research on coercive isomorphism has concentrated on the European Commission. A specific example in the context of European integration is the reaction of European institutions to the alleged legitimacy deficit of their policy processes. These criticisms, voiced by European societies through negative referenda outcomes, led to the introduction of a number of new democratic instruments at the European level. According to research based on sociological institutionalist perspectives, the concept of legitimacy or its deficit must be understood as an inter-subjective property that 'operates through individuals via cognitive scripts' (Goetze and Rittberger 2010: 37; Bartolini 2005). It thus helps to understand that the legitimacy deficit is not an unchangeable fact but a shared cognitive framework that structures agents' attitudes in policy-making processes. Another empirical example of this approach can be found in studies on the collective institutional cultures. For instance, controversies inside the European Commission, the European Parliament or agencies have been explained through the establishment of divergent collective values or cognitive frames which make the defence of specific positions possible (Christiansen and Tonra 2004; Cini 1996; Fouilleux 2004; Jachtenfuchs 2001).

Finally, mimesis, a variant of isomorphism, is thought to occur mostly through the migration of professionals from one organization to another. In a context of uncertainty and limited rationality, institutions have a tendency to imitate one another. Sociological institutionalism has convincingly shown that research in this area is interested in the transfer of institutional forms such as independent agencies or the European Central Bank, from the national to the European level (Wonka and Rittberger 2011). Thus, common understandings are established in policy-making through processes of emulation and diffusion, and, in fact, diminishing issue complexity.

Socialization and learning

Similar to the hypotheses developed by the mimesis aspect of sociological institutionalism, but without the identification of a clear role model as offered by
sociological institutionalist perspectives, socialization and learning approaches
look for evidence of socialization within the European integration process
(Checkel 1999; 2001; 2003; 2005; 2006; Zürn and Checkel 2005). Socialization occurs when norms, worldviews, collective understandings are internalized,
and subsequently are codified by a group of actors (Risse 2009; Schimmelfennig
2000).

Based on this assumption, a large number of analyses have been carried out on
the socializing role of European institutions. If a large proportion of policy outcomes results from exchanges between actors and can be understood as strategic
bargaining, certain processes analysed from this viewpoint do not make any sense.

> Constitutive dynamics of social learning, socialization, routinization and nor-
> mative diffusion, all of which address fundamental issues of agent identity and
> interests, are not adequately captured by strategic exchange or other models
> adhering to strict forms of methodological individualism. (Checkel 1999:
> 545)

The central research object here is not so much the construction of a European
identity in the broader sense. Instead, the research concentrates on the influence
the collective acceptance of certain standards of behaviour exerts on the policy-
making processes (Beyers 2005; Checkel 2001; Hooghe 2005; Tallberg 2002).

Sympathetic critiques of this research insist on the fact that learning and
socialization processes are phenomena which must be rigorously studied in
order to understand the moment at which a norm becomes a general reference
and is not just an idea or ideological position of one single individual (see also
Radaelli and Dunlop 2013; Saurugger 2010). Empirical research mainly concentrates on specific professional groups active in the EU realm, such as European civil servants, the committee of permanent representatives (COREPER),
members of interest groups (Checkel 2003; Hooghe 2000, 2005; Lewis 2005,
2008), or specific policy fields such as those in which the Open Method of
Co-ordination (OMC) is particularly prominent: gender mainstreaming; life-
long learning flexicurity; or activation (Zeitlin 2005). Through continuous
interaction, actors in groups of actors share a number of common values,
which, in turn, influence their positions in decision-making processes.

On the one hand, this conceptualization of learning has two advantages. First
of all, it shows that certain actors do not only succeed in imposing their
interpretation of social phenomena or their norms as hegemonies because
they have the necessary authority or because a window of opportunity opens
up. Their arguments are persuasive because they have managed to create a
common understanding of a problem and thus hold a legitimate position
through the broader social context in which they are embedded (Dimitrova
and Rhinard 2005; Jobert and Muller 1987).

The second advantage is the ability to integrate one of the major challenges of research into European integration, i.e., thinking about the multitude of levels where reality is constructed. Reality is constructed by the individual, the group to which it belongs, the media or, more generally, the messages that are transmitted on several levels: locally; regionally; nationally; Europe-wide; or more internationally. Issue complexity, which has been identified as a problem in the collection, seems to decrease in the fields where socialization occurs.

However, one of the main questions that remains is to understand why a large number of bargaining processes still seem not based on a shared understanding of the problem (i.e., the Economic and Monetary Union [EMU] crisis, the reform of the Common Agricultural Policy, or the budget negotiations), although governmental representatives have co-operated for more than 50 years in Brussels. Can the explanation be found on the level of analysis? In other words, can we observe learning and socialization processes in which common worldviews are constructed only in small and very technical groups, whereas intergovernmental bargaining remains focused on national collective understandings?

Discursive institutionalism

A relatively new form of constructivist institutionalism applied to public policy studies developed at the end of the 1990s. It is summarized by Vivien Schmidt under the label of discursive institutionalism (Schmidt 2008; for first conceptualizations, see Fairclough 1992; Hay 2004; Hay and Rosamond 2002; Peters 2005). Discursive institutionalism investigates changes of paradigm and reference sets of public policies through ideas which are perceived as central variables of research.

While ideas are still identified as mechanisms of political change, discursive institutionalism attempts to solve the causality question: precisely how do ideas influence public policies? The main question is thus not how discursive practices make certain EU norms possible in the first place, as post-positivists would ask (Diez 1999), but how worldviews influence policy outcomes. The answer to this second question is straightforward: ideas require the existence of a vehicle or a carrier. Discourse is identified as the main instrument of change. In this logic it is important to focus on the content of ideas and the interactive process which brings them to a head and which communicates them to the public. Thus, discursive institutionalism traces the process from the emergence of ideas, through their dissemination and finally their legitimization (Wincott 2004).

For instance, at the European Union level, the European Commission has attempted to increasingly build up a discourse to legitimize its policies and reforms to compensate for the alleged democratic deficit the EU has been accused of since the beginning of the 1990s (Fouilleux 2004). While the German and French attempts to reform their telecommunications policy were enforced by discourse that directly referred to EU institutional requirements, the reform in French immigration policy did not refer to European pressure (Geddes and Guiraudon 2004; Thatcher 2004).

The problem of making sense and understanding the impact of issue complexity of EU policy-making on policy outcomes here is addressed by concentrating on actors' discourses. Discursive institutionalism is more a research method than a conceptual framework: it attempts to measure how worldviews, ideas, collective understandings make their way into policy outcomes.

The problem the approach faces is twofold: to determine whether discourse really can be the independent variable; and to distinguish between ideas and strategies. As with sociological institutionalism, establishing causal links between the different phenomena is extremely difficult. The solution offered by discursive institutionalism is thus to concentrate on correlations between variables instead of insisting on causality (Schmidt and Radaelli 2004).

The second difficulty – differentiating between ideas and strategies in discourse – has been tackled head-on by actor-centred constructivists, who do not distinguish between ideas and strategies but argue that ideas, as well as any other argument, can be used strategically in a negotiation.

Actor-centred constructivism

The main problem when using one of the three approaches presented above is the fact that power relations and the strategic behaviour of policy agents somehow seem secondary, if they appear at all.

Since the end of the 1990s, a group of scholars has attempted to accommodate the limits of previous constructivist conceptualizations of EU politics, referring to the fact that the strategic considerations of the actors involved were largely ignored in constructivist approaches. Whilst these researchers agree with the general constructivist assumption on the fact that the individual ideas and beliefs of an actor are constructed, they emphasize the importance of taking into account *how specific actors use these ideas*. The central question to which actor-centred constructivism seeks to find an answer is to understand how precisely ideas count in policy outcomes. It is interesting to underline here that actor-centred constructivists rather consistently use the term 'ideas' throughout their research. Ideas are considered to be explanatory factors in their own right. But as Mark Blyth notes, constructivist perspectives – which include in our case in particular socialization and learning approaches as well as discursive institutionalism – have for too long opposed interests and ideas and considered them to be radically different and unrelated concepts (Blyth 2002; see also McNamara 2006).

How do ideas frame interests, and how can one describe the practices of actors and the development of public policy through this framing process? When and why, for example, do European public officials evoke the neoliberal paradigm in their messages, and when and why does this idea not find its way into official documents and discourse? These questions lead to identifying the agents who pay attention to certain ideas and not to others, as well as the reasons why certain decisions are made at a specific period and not at another (Zahariadis 2008). In other words:

> Since structures do not come with an instruction sheet, economic ideas make such an institutional resolution possible by providing the authoritative diagnosis as to what a crisis actually is and when a given situation actually constitutes a crisis. They diagnose 'what has gone wrong' and 'what is to be done'. (Blyth 2002: 10; see also Hay 1999, 2004)

Ideas are considered as malleable objects – they can be used for strategic purposes. The purely rhetorical use of these notions underestimates the forms of mobilization and instrumentalization to which these frames have been subject (Surel 2000). It is, in a certain sense, rather trivial to say that these strategies are socially constructed. However, in saying this, it is important to understand that actors must create broad coalitions around common strategies in order to carry out major reforms.

Research based on this perspective is particularly important in the field of the European political economy. The main question here is why and how a convergence of beliefs around economic and political solutions to specific European problems has emerged (Abdelal *et al.* 2010; Berman 1998; Blyth 2002; Clift and Woll 2012; Hall 1993; Jabko 2006, 2010; McNamara 1998, 2006; Meyer and Strickman 2011; Parsons 2002; Woll 2008).

While these scholars develop different hypotheses and might not be comfortable with being called actor-centred constructivists, they agree on the basic assumption that, even if the international environment confronts political leaders with a set of challenges, this does not automatically mean that the 'correct' or 'best' answer, which, without doubt, would solve the problem, will be forthcoming. However, where these authors differ is in the degree of independence the carriers of ideas have. For one group of scholars, the understanding of economic, political and social challenges, their interpretation and their analysis is filtered by cultural and ideal structures in which political actors operate. In order to be visible, ideas must serve the interest of the dominant actors by strengthening their position in the game (Béland 2009; Hall 1993; McNamara 1998; Parsons 2002). Another group considers ideas as weapons that can be used quite independently from the position of the actor itself (Blyth 2002; Jabko 2006).

However, the difficulty of showing the empirical influence of ideas remains. One of the problems is to be found in the dichotomic (Janus-faced) nature of ideas (Parsons 2002). Sometimes the beliefs of actors guide their actions and sometimes perceived beliefs only rationalize strategies that can be chosen for other reasons. Empirically distinguishing between the two situations is rather difficult and can only be done by establishing causality. This causality allows the sequence of decisions and paradigm changes to be made visible.

Thus, actor-centred constructivism introduces sociological methods, concentrating on the study of individual actors or groups of actors, which are aimed to help in the understanding of the power games that take place between actors in public policy. Craig Parsons, in particular, argues that, in order to observe the influence of ideas, it is crucial to consider the agenda-setting power of the actor in question. In his analysis of the success of integration ideology in relation to the confederal or intergovernmental model developed by the 'founding fathers' of European integration, Parsons offers a micro-sociological study of French debates on this issue, as well as of the interactions between European partners in the 1950s (Parsons 2002).

The analysis of the intensified European economic regional integration process starting from the 1980s uses a similar research design (Jabko 2006). Here European integration is studied from the angle of economic governance. The observation is based on the dual economic and political change in Europe and on the definition of a political strategy of 'market gain' developed by European actors and, in particular, the European Commission. This strategy is based on the idea of a common market, a concept which is sufficiently multi-tasking to bring together all the European actors' ideologies around a single project: the construction of the single market and the Economic and Monetary Union, the driving force behind the European Commission's political strategy. This 'silent revolution' in Europe over time brought together a broad coalition of European actors. Through the use of what he calls 'strategic constructivism', Jabko emphasizes two paradoxical aspects of the European Union: the parallel emergence of intergovernmental economic governance; and the strengthening of powers at the European level. According to Jabko, the European Union is not just a marketing tool serving neoliberal ideologies. The European Commission is an active agent developing a specific understanding of neoliberalism not as a homogenous paradigm but a discursive notion allowing for different interpretations and strategies guiding economic policies.

Actor-centred and, more precisely, 'strategic constructivism' attempts to tackle critiques expressed by opponents of constructivist approaches focusing, on the one hand, on who the carriers of ideas and norms are, and on the other, how their power relations shape the policy outcomes under scrutiny. Economically rationalist thinking is brought back into the analysis and linked to the use actors make of these ideas. Agents are purposeful actors, embedded in ideational structures, which they use according to their interests.

Actor-centred constructivism thus allows us to deal particularly well with two issues found in EU policy-making in particular: on the one hand, the complexity of policy-making processes; on the other, legitimation issues. There are, however, a number of pitfalls that actor-centred constructivists might take into account when further developing their research.

Complexity

The combination of a constructivist and rationalist research design makes actor-centred or 'strategic' constructivist perspectives particularly interesting in public policy studies aimed at explaining the EU, given the complexity of decision-making at this level. As stated in the introduction, actors often lack a clear and well-articulated set of preferences in policy processes, and have contradictory preferences which are embedded in specific values and world views.

While these characteristics are central elements in the analysis of the complexity of contemporary societies in general, the notion of complexity seen by actor-centred constructivists goes beyond the difference in positions or interests. While these differences undoubtedly exist, these scholars question the origin of these differences and find them in different world views of social groups. Contemporary social systems, which are both agents of social change through public policies and addressees of these changes, are characterized through functional differentiation. Agents evolve in different subsystems at the same time and their interests are therefore influenced by a multitude of values and ideas.

All constructivist perspectives seem at first sight particularly apt to address the problems of issue complexity that arise in contemporary systems of governance, and more particularly in the EU. As underlined in Zahariadis's introduction to this collection, issue complexity makes agreements between policy-makers difficult, not only because more people need to agree but also because decision-makers will be more likely to contest the framing of the debate. Actor-centred constructivists aim to uncover rather that to assume rationality of policy agents in their research.

While the first generations of constructivist approaches to EU studies developed frameworks to explain issue complexity more than institutional complexity in the EU, the development of actor-centred constructivism has allowed for reintroducing tools that address this issue. Higher institutional complexity gives rise to potential conflict. A high number of actors with overlapping and often conflicting competencies increase the possibility of power struggles for control of agendas and resources.

At the same time, this new generation of constructivist perspectives continues to include ideas and world views as central causal factors in the explanation of the decision-making processes. However, they insist on the fact that ideas, worldviews or norms do not exist independently from the users of these ideas and the institutional conditions in which they are embedded. Thus, world views, norms or ideas 'do not float freely' as Thomas Risse-Kappen (1994) has so pertinently observed. One of the main problems here is the question of methodology. How shall we analyse the interdependence between ideas and interests, both of them more generally embedded in specific worldviews?

Legitimation

Beyond the treatment of the complexity of social systems, constructivist approaches are equally useful to explain legitimation strategies actors pursue in policy-making processes. This is important, as in both political and academic debates the question of legitimate and accountable governance in the European Union has become a crucial issue since the mid-1990s. The influence of ideas, of 'world views', of 'ways of seeing things', of frames or more generally of representations is at the centre of these approaches. In this sense, public policy is understood as the result of the interaction between individuals whose interests are not only based on a rational cost–benefit calculation, but must be understood as something that is embedded in specific social representations, values and norms in which the actor evolves. General constructivist approaches in public policy aim at helping us understand why some proposals have more legitimacy in a debate than others at a given time:

> Politicians, officials, the spokesmen for societal interests, and policy experts all operate within the terms of political discourse that are current in the nation at a given time, and the terms of political discourse generally have a specific configuration that lends representative legitimacy to some social interests more than others, delineates the accepted boundaries of state action, associates contemporary political developments with particular interpretations of national history, and defines the context in which many issues will be understood. (Hall 1993: 289; see also Surel 2000)

This conceptualization does not exclude behaviour based on cost and benefit analysis. However, this attitude only occurs when actors have chosen the instruments available to them in order to pursue a specific objective. Again, and this seems somewhat circular, these objectives, however, are influenced through cognitive and normative frames available to them. In this sense, 'actors always perceive the world through a lens consisting of their pre-existing beliefs' (Sabatier 1998: 109). These pre-existing beliefs, as Sabatier calls them, norms or cognitive frames are not homogenous. Conflict amongst actors within these frames constantly occurs, as well as amongst actors who have adopted different frames in negotiations leading to public policies. These conflicts thus allow us to explain why policies change, instead of insisting on their normative embeddedness and their ensuing static character.

This understanding of ideas and cognitive frames, particularly developed in constructivist approaches, allows the legitimacy of public policies to be conceptualized differently. Legitimacy thus is no longer an absolute value but must be understood in the light of a permanent framing process in which different ideas about legitimacy confront each other: the legitimacy of public policies becomes the process of legitimation of public policies (Jobert and Muller 1987). This research field has gained in importance since the beginning of the 1990s, when the debate on the democratic deficit of the European Union became an important issue. Why European and domestic actors adopt positions in the European debate was analysed in the light of their understanding of the European democratic space and not only as a cost–benefit attitude. It is here where strategic constructivism encounters a limit: if ideas become purely a weapon (Blyth 2002) or a strategic tool (Jabko 2006), then the legitimacy of a policy process is nothing more than a lure. It is methodologically challenging to analyse at the same time the influence of ideas as a strategic tool and the influence of the political, social or economic context in which these ideas occur. The link between the logic of consequentialism and the logic of appropriateness which is so well argued for by strategic constructivists, however, is methodologically difficult to realize. Is there a way forward to solve these issues?

CONCLUSION: FUTURE AGENDAS

We have seen that constructivist approaches in public policy are particularly well suited to explaining the complexity of the policy process. While the first generation of constructivist approaches (sociological and discursive institutionalism, as well as socialization and learning) in EU public policy helped in particular to understand the *issue* complexity of European policies, actor-centred constructivism allowed the introduction of tools to conceptualize *institutional* complexity. The assumption that ideas could be used strategically by EU agents constitutes an extremely useful instrument to overcome the artificial dichotomy between the logic of appropriateness and the logic of consequentialism. This becomes particularly clear when we think about the German and French governments' attempts to establish an economic government in the European Union as an answer to the economic and financial crises since 2009. Their positions are both embedded in their national history and influenced by their economic preferences in a globalized market.

The continued insistence of constructivist accounts in general on the multiplicity of actors' positions framed by their institutional, cognitive or cultural embeddeddness, the fact that policy outcomes are not based exclusively on economic rational calculations, or, finally, the significant role played by the socialization processes of actors on policy outcomes helps to better understand policy processes.

The crucial role played by the contextualization of processes, i.e., the fact that they are embedded in a certain social, political or economic context, based on an important number of variables that cannot be reduced to a simple linearity between interests and outcomes, advocated by constructivist approaches, leads to a rather detailed research protocol and precise statements on policy processes.

However, there are a number of challenges with which constructivist approaches in EU public policy are confronted:

- Methodological challenges referring to the fact that research based on microsociological studies or even detailed case studies a number of constructivist scholars call for (see Béland 2009) do not seem entirely sufficient to understand the extent to which the embeddedness of actors explains their positions in policy negotiations, or the final policy outcome. Understanding the attitudes of specific Directorates-General (DGs) or groups of actors in policymaking does not help us to understand the EU integration process in general. It helps us to understand details, but not in which direction the European integration process might be heading in general. Which macrosociological worldviews (if there are any) influence the policy results? And what does this mean for a supranational governance system in the global context?

- The establishment of a correlation between ideas, norms or world views and policy outcomes is still not entirely convincing. The central criticism voiced by Andrew Moravcsik (1999), that ideas constantly float around (albeit not freely) in political as well as policy processes and that it is therefore vain to try to understand these often contradictory variables which do not significantly influence policy outcomes, still echoes in constructivist research. While strategic constructivists attempt to introduce economically rational elements in their embeddedness research, other constructivist approaches insist on the long-term and learning factors in order to explain policy outcomes. Norms, ideas, informal institutions, belief systems or world views are, however, extremely difficult to define and thus to operationalize in order to understand their influence in the policy process.
- Finally, some constructivist public policy approaches are in danger of becoming so concentrated with small-scale case studies that they forget to be interested in the bigger picture of European integration. This is particularly true of sociological and discursive institutionalist frameworks which might gain in importance if they were to address larger questions than the precise influence of socialization or of discourse on specific policy outcomes. Thus, understanding the discourse of one specific expert group in one policy area, such as mad cow disease, will only inform us on the use of ideas and norms in one historically contingent negotiation process at the EU level. Widening the research scope of these approaches might lead to more general comments and less evidence-based research, as norms, ideas or worldviews can be catch-all terms if not precisely defined.

Thus, the future agenda of constructivist approaches calls for a large-scale empirical research programme in which norms, rules, world views and cognitive frameworks are clearly defined and in which correlations between these views and policy outcomes can be more clearly established. Large-scale research can take two forms. First, as a longitudinal analysis presenting a history of the EU in which policy processes, beyond the moments of crisis, such as treaty negotiations, are analysed. Second, as a research design that concentrates on a comparison, based on a combination of qualitative and quantitative research methods (i.e., Ragin 1987), between specific policy areas which are analysed in detail. Both research designs would go beyond pure description. Research based on actor-centred or strategic constructivism seems, for the time being, most promising in this respect, as it allows both strategic thinking and cognitive contextualization to be taken into account.

Biographical note: Sabine Saurugger is Professor of Politics at Sciences Po Grenoble, and member of the Institut universitaire de France.

ACKNOWLEDGEMENTS

I wish to thank Nikolaos Zahariadis, the participants of the EUSA panel on Theories of the EU Policy Process, and the anonymous reviewers for their helpful comments and constructive criticism on early drafts. The research was supported by a fellowship at the Institut universitaire de France (IUF).

NOTE

1 While all these terms have very specific definitions, they are used by a majority of constructivist approaches dealt with in this article as synonymous. A detailed differentiation would go way beyond the scope of this article.

REFERENCES

Abdelal, R., Blyth, M. and Parsons, C. (2010) *Constructing the International Economy*, Ithaca, NY: Cornell University Press.

Bartolini, S. (2005) *Restructuring Europe*, Oxford: Oxford University Press.

Béland, D. (2009) 'Ideas, institutions, and policy change', *Journal of European Public Policy* 16(5): 701–18.

Béland, D. and Cox, R.H. (eds) (2011) *Ideas and Politics in Social Science Research*, Oxford: Oxford University Press.

Berger, P. and Luckmann, T. (1966) *The Social Construction of Reality*, New York: Doubleday.

Berman, S. (1998) *The Primacy of Politics: Social Democracy and the Making of Europe's Twentieth Century*, New York: Cambridge University Press.

Beyers, J. (2005) 'Multiple embeddedness and socialization in Europe: the case of Council officials', *International Organization* 59(4): 899–936.

Blyth, M. (1997) '"Any more bright ideas?" The ideational turn in comparative political economy', *Comparative Politics* 29(2): 229–50.

Blyth, M. (2002) *The Great Transformation: Economic Ideas and Institutional Change in the 20th century*, Cambridge: Cambridge University Press.

Checkel, J. (1993) 'Ideas, institutions and the Gorbachev foreign policy revolution', *World Politics* 45(2): 271–300.

Checkel, J. (1999) 'Social construction and integration', *Journal of European Public Policy* 6(4): 545–60.

Checkel, J. (2001) 'Why comply? Social learning and European identity change', *International Organization* 55(3): 553–88.

Checkel, J. (2003) '"Going native" in Europe? Theorizing social interaction in European institutions', *Comparative Political Studies* 36(1–2): 209–31.

Checkel, J. (2005) 'International institutions and socialization in Europe: introduction and framework', *International Organization* 59: 801–26.

Checkel, J. (2006) Constructivist approaches to European integration, ARENA Working Paper, no. 6, available at http://www.sv.uio.no/arena/english/research/publications/arena-publications/workingpapers/working-papers2006/wp06_06.xml (accessed 20 September 2012).

Christiansen, T., Joergensen, K.E. and Wiener, A. (1999) 'The social construction of Europe', *Journal of European Public Policy* 6(4): 528–44.

Christiansen, T. and Tonra, B. (eds) (2004) *Rethinking European Union Foreign Policy*, Manchester: Manchester University Press.

Cini, C. (1996) *The European Commission: Leadership, Organization and Culture in the EU Administration*, Manchester: Manchester University Press.

Clift, B. and Woll, C. (2012) 'Economic patriotism: reinventing control over open markets', *Journal of European Public Policy* 19(3): 307–23.

Cox, R. (2001) 'The way ahead: towards a new ontology of world order', in R.W. Jones (ed.), *Critical Theory and World Politics*, Boulder, CO: Lynne Rienner, pp. 45–60.

Culpepper, P. (2008) 'The politics of common knowledge: ideas and institutional change in wage bargaining', *International Organization* 62(1): 1–33.

Diez, T. (1999) 'Speaking "Europe": the politics of integration discourse', *Journal of European Public Policy* 6(4): 598–613.

DiMaggio, P.J. and Powell, W.A. (eds) (1991) *The New Institutionalism in Organizational Analysis*, Chicago and London: University of Chicago Press.

Dimitrova, A. and Rhinard, M. (2005) 'The power of norms in the transposition of EU directives', *European Integration Online Papers* 9(16), available at http://eiop.or.at/eiop/texte/2005-016a.htm (accessed 9 April 2013).

Eilstrup-Sangiovanni, M. (2006) *Debates on European Integration. A Reader*, Basingstoke: Palgrave.

Elster, J. (1989) *Nuts and Bolts for the Social Sciences*, Cambridge: Cambridge University Press.

Fairclough, N. (1992) *Discourse and Social Change*, Cambridge: Polity Press.

Fischer, F. (2003) *Reframing Public Policy: Discursive Politics and Deliberative Practices*, Oxford: Oxford University Press.

Fouilleux, E. (2004) 'CAP reform and multilateral trade negotiations: another view on discourse efficiency', *West European Politics* 27(2): 235–55.

Geddes, A. and Guiraudon, V. (2004) 'The emergence of a European policy paradigm', *West European Politics* 27(2): 334–53.

Genyies, W. and Smyrl, M. (2008) *Elites, Ideas, and the Evolution of Public Policy*, Houndsmills: Basingstoke, Palgrave.

Goetze, S. and Rittberger, B. (2010) 'A matter of habit? The sociological foundations of empowering the European Parliament', *Comparative European Politics* 8(1): 37–54.

Gofas, A. and Hay, C. (2010) 'The ideational turn and the persistence of perennial dualisms', in A. Gofas and C. Hay (eds), *The Role of Ideas in Political Analysis: A Portrait of Contemporary Debates*, London: Routledge, pp. 13–55.

Goldstein, J. and Keohane, R. (eds) (1993) *Ideas and Foreign Policy : Beliefs, Institutions and Political Change*, Ithaca, NY: Cornell University Press.

Hall, P. (1993) 'Policy paradigms, social learning and the state. The case of economic policy-making in Britain', *Comparative Politics* 25(3): 275–96.

Hay, C. (1999) 'Crisis and the structural transformation of the state. Integrating processes of change', *British Journal of Politics and International Relations* 1(3): 317–44.

Hay, C. (2004) 'Ideas, interests, and institutions in the comparative political economy of great transformations', *Review of International Political Economy* 11(1): 204–26.

Hay, C. and Rosamond, B. (2002) 'Globalization, European integration and the discursive construction of economic imperatives', *Journal of European Public Policy* 9(2): 147–67.

Hooghe, L. (2000) 'Euro-socialists or Euro-marketeers? Contention about European capitalism among senior Commission officials', *Journal of Politics* 62(2): 430–54.

Hooghe, L. (2005) 'Several roads lead to international norms, but few via international socialization: a case study of the European Commission', *International Organization* 59(4): 861–98.

Jabko, N. (2006) *Playing the Market*, Ithaca, NY, and London: Cornell University Press.

Jabko, N. (2010) 'The hidden face of the euro', *Journal of European Public Policy* 17(3): 318–34.

Jachtenfuchs, M. (2001) 'The governance approach to European integration', *Journal of Common Market Studies* 39(3): 249–64.

Jobert, B. and Muller, P. (1987) *L'Etat en action. Politiques publiques et coropratismes*, Paris: Presses universitaires de France.

Lewis, J. (2005) 'The Janus face of Brussels: socialization and everyday decision making in the EU', *International Organization* 59(4): 937–71.

Lewis, J. (2008) 'Strategic bargaining, norms and deliberation: modes of action in the Council of the European Union', in D. Naurin and H. Wallace (eds), *Unveiling the Council: Games Governments Play in Brussels*, Houndmills: Palgrave Macmillan, pp. 165–84.

March, J.G. and Olsen, J.P. (1984) 'The new institutionalism: organizational factors in political life', *American Political Science Review* 78: 734–49.

March, J.G. and Olsen, J.P. (1989) *Rediscovering Institutions*, New York: Free Press.

March, J.G. and Olsen, J.P. (1998) 'The institutional dynamics of international political order', *International Organization* 52(4): 943–69.

March, J.G. and Olsen, J.P. (2004) The logic of appropriateness, Arena Working Papers, WP 04/09, http://www.sv.uio.no/arena/english/research/publications/arena-publications/workingpapers/working-papers2004/04_09.xml (accessed 19 September 2012).

McNamara, K. (1998) *The Currency of Ideas, Monetary Politics in the European Union*, Ithaca, NY, and London: Cornell University Press.

McNamara, K. (2006) 'Economic governance, ideas and EMU: what currency does policy consensus have today?' *Journal of Common Market Studies* 44(4): 803–21.

Meyer, C.O. and Strickman, E. (2011) 'Solidifying constructivism: how material and ideational factors interact in European defence', *Journal of Common Market Studies* 49(1): 61–81.

Moravcsik, A. (1999) 'Is something rotten in the state of Denmark? Constructivism and European integration', *Journal of European Public Policy* 6(5): 669–81.

Mueller, D.C. (2003) *Public Choice III*, Cambridge: Cambridge University Press.

Ostrom, O. (1999) 'Institutional rational choice. an assessment of the institutional analysis and development framework', in P.A. Sabatier (ed.), *Theories of the Policy Process*, Boulder, CO: Westview Press, pp. 35–71.

Parsons, C. (2002) 'Showing ideas as causes: the origins of the European Union', *International Organization* 55(1): 47–84.

Parsons, C. (2010) 'How – and how much – are sociological approaches to the EU distinctive?' *Comparative European Politics* 8(1): 143–59.

Peters, B.G. (2005) *Institutional Theory in Political Science: The New Institutionalism*, London: Continuum.

Ragin, C.C. (1987) *The Comparative Method: Moving beyond Qualitative and Quantitative Strategies*, Berkeley, Los Angeles, CA, and London: University of California Press.

Radaelli, C. and Dunlop, C. (2013) 'Learning in the European Union: theoretical lenses and meta-theory', *Journal of European Public Policy* 20(6), doi: 10.1080/13501763.2013.781832.

Risse, T. (2004) 'Social constructivism and European integration', in A. Wiener and T. Diez (eds), *European Integration Theory*, Oxford: Oxford University Press, pp. 159–76.

Risse, T. (2009) 'Social constructivism and European integration', in A. Wiener and T. Diez (eds), *European Integration Theory*, Oxford: Oxford University Press, pp. 159–76.

Risse-Kappen, T. (1994) 'Ideas do not float freely: transnational coalitions, domestic structures and the end of the Cold War', *International Organization* 48(2): 185–214.

Rosamond, B. (2000) *Theories of European Integration*, Basingstoke, Palgrave.

Sabatier, P. (1998) 'The advocacy coalition framework: revisions and relevance for Europe', *Journal of European Public Policy* 5(1): 93–130.

Saurugger, S. (2010) 'The social construction of the participatory turn: the emergence of a norm in the European Union', *European Journal of Political Research* 49(4): 471–95.

Schimmelfennig, F. (2000) 'International sozialisation in the new Europe: rational action in an institutional environment', *European Journal of International Relations* 6(1): 109–39.

Schmidt, V.A. (2008) 'Discursive Institutionalism: The Explanatory Power of Ideas and Discourses', *Annual Review of Political Science* 11: 303–26.

Schmidt, V. and Radaelli, C. (2004) 'Conclusions', *West European Politics* 27(2): 364–79.

Surel, Y. (2000) 'The role of cognitive and normative frames in policy making', *Journal of European Public Policy* 7(4): 495–512.

Tallberg, J. (2002) 'Paths to compliance: enforcement, management and the European Union', *International Organization* 56(3): 609–44.

Thatcher, M. (2004) 'Winners and losers in Europeanization: reforming the national regulation of telecommunications', *West European Politics* 27(2): 284–309.

Wendt, A. (1999) *Social Theory of International Politics*, Cambridge: Cambridge University Press.

Wincott, D. (2004) 'Policy change and discourse in Europe: can the EU make a square meal out of a stew of paradox?' *West European Politics* 27(4): 354–63.

Woll, C. (2008) *Firm Interests: How Governments Shape Business Lobbying on Global Trade*, New York: Cornell University Press.

Wonka, A. and Rittberger, B. (2011) 'Perspectives on EU governance: an empirical assessment of the political attitudes of EU agency professionals', *Journal of European Public Policy* 18(6): 888–908.

Zahariadis, N. (1999) 'Ambiguity, times and multiples treams', in P.A. Sabatier (ed.), *Theories of the Policy Process: Theoretical Lenses on Public Policy*. Boulder, CO: Westview Press, pp. 73–93.

Zahariadis, N. (2003) *Ambiguity and Choice in Public Policy, Political Decision Making in Modern Democracies*, Washington, DC: Georgetown University Press.

Zahariadis, N. (2008) 'Europeanization as program implementation: effective and democratic?' *Journal of Comparative Policy Analysis* 10(3): 221–38.

Zahariadis, N. (2013) 'Building better frameworks of the European Union's policy process, *Journal of European Public Policy* 20(6), doi: 10.1080/13501763.2013.781815.

Zeitlin, J. (2005) 'Conclusion', in J. Zeitlin and P. Pochet (eds), *The Open Method of Coordinationin Action*, Brussels: PIE Peter Lang, pp. 447–503.

Zürn, M. and Checkel, J.T. (2005) 'Getting socialized to build bridges: constructivism and rationalism, Europe and the nation state', *International Organization* 59(4): 1045–79.

A normative power Europe framework of transnational policy formation

Vicki Birchfield

ABSTRACT Since introduced by Ian Manners in 2002, 'normative power Europe' (NPE), has emerged as one of the most widely debated approaches in European Studies. While critiques persist, NPE continues to be innovatively applied by scholars exploring the role of the European Union as a global actor. This contribution aims to position NPE scholarship away from 'essentialist' theoretical debates and towards its use as an analytical apparatus for examining transnational policy formation. Illustrating *why* NPE may be recast as a policy framework, it offers an exposition of its key concepts and theoretical underpinnings and presents a set of criteria against which it may be empirically assessed. Turning to *how* NPE operates as a policy framework, a survey and evaluation of NPE scholarship is provided as well as a comparison with other approaches and an overview of the strengths and limitations of the NPE framework for understanding the EU's policy process.

One decade ago, in a 2002 article published in the *Journal of Common Market Studies*, Ian Manners introduced the concept of 'normative power Europe' (NPE), which quickly became one of the most widely debated approaches to understanding the international identity and external actions of the European Union (EU). Just four years later, Manners offered a response to critics and a reappraisal of his original formulation in a special issue of the *Journal of European Public Policy* (*JEPP*). Subsequently, in a virtual special issue devoted exclusively to recent NPE scholarship, Manners claimed that: 'The normative power approach is emerging as a holistic research programme with the potential to cross both policy and disciplinary boundaries in the study of the EU's status in, and relations with, the rest of the world.'[1] It is worth pointing out that Manners acknowledged that this journal – *JEPP* – has published more highly cited articles on NPE than any other academic journal and thus had become 'a central point of reference for normative power research and debate in a wide variety of public policy areas.'[2] It is somewhat paradoxical that a journal explicitly oriented toward research on public policy has generated so much debate and commentary on an approach that might not readily be identified as a policy framework *per se*. However, as this contribution argues, Manners's original articulation as well as much of the ensuing scholarship illustrate that NPE can and should be deployed as an analytical framework of the EU policy process.

There are two compelling justifications for considering the NPE framework and its contributions to advancing knowledge of the EU policy process. First, NPE was originally – (and for some scholars still), remains primarily – geared towards understanding what kind of actor the European Union is in terms of its increasingly collective role in the international system. Therefore, the extent to which the NPE framework places ontological questions front and center distinguishes it from most other approaches (with the possible exception of constructivism) that are specifically enlisted to explain the EU policy-making process. Paradoxically, this tendency leads some to view NPE as overly essentialist, despite the emphatic argument by Manners and Whitman to the contrary (2003) and the insistence on the non-essentialist, fluid and relational aspects of the EU's complex identity (see especially Whitman 2011b: 10–11). Second, whereas most approaches to EU policy-making are predominantly borrowed from frameworks aimed at understanding national level policy-making processes, NPE is an EU specific framework. As NPE was developed intentionally as a lens through which to understand the EU's external actions and foreign policies, the approach should yield distinctive insights into the policy-making process in a very specific, albeit multidimensional and complex policy domain.

To tackle the question of 'why' NPE can indeed be employed as a policy framework, it is important to revisit Manners's original conceptualization of normative power:

> The concept of normative power is an attempt to suggest that not only is the EU constructed on a normative basis, but importantly that this predisposes it to act in a normative way in world politics. It is built on the crucial and usually overlooked observation that the most important factor shaping the international role of the EU is not what it does or what it says, but what it is. Thus, my presentation of the EU as a normative power has an ontological quality to it – that the EU can be *conceptualized* as a changer of norms in the international system; a positivist quantity to it – that the EU *acts* to change norms in the international system; and a normative quality to it – that the EU *should* act to extend its norms into the international system. (Manners 2002: 252; emphasis original)

Contained in this widely cited paragraph are two distinct statements that reveal why NPE remains an enigma or a confusing debate to some and yet, according to a growing number of its interlocutors (see Whitman 2011), it has the capacity for generating new theoretical and empirical insights into the study of the European Union. The two statements in a sense represent a variation on the dialectic of being and becoming. First, Manners asserts that what is most salient about the EU's international role is not what it does or says but 'what it is'. This suggests that the concept really is meant to affirm the *sui generis*[3] character of the EU as a unique and different kind of international actor, and underscores that what we must pay attention to this elemental feature of the EU's identity rather than solely focusing on its behavior. The second statement, however, draws our mind back to the realm of action, particularly where Manners asserts the 'positivist' dimension – i.e., that the EU *acts* to change norms in the international system. We will return to these ontological, positive and normative specifications below in the discussion of assessment criteria.

It is often neglected that Manners devoted considerable effort in his original article to proffering an empirical analysis and evidence of the concept of normative power Europe by tracing how the EU and its member states actively mobilize on behalf of one of its core norms – human rights – and its international policy of seeking the abolition of the death penalty worldwide. The EU employs lobbying tactics actively within the United States and elsewhere to end capital punishment and engages a variety of different policy instruments to pursue this objective. Therefore, it is clear, despite misinterpretations to the contrary, that the idea of normative power Europe was intended not merely as a conceptual or theoretical exercise, but indeed had as an object of inquiry the assessment of the EU's external actions and policies.

As the introduction to the aforementioned *JEPP* virtual issue highlighted: 'Within this research programme, the greatest challenges involve analysing both the causal and constitutive effects of EU principles, actions and impact in world politics.'[4] The present contribution heeds this call by articulating the merits of the NPE approach as a valid framework for understanding the EU's policy-making process.

NORMATIVE POWER EUROPE: FROM THEORETICAL CONCEPT TO POLICY FRAMEWORK

In seeking to understand policy formation in the context of a complex transnational decision making arena like the European Union, where both national and community level interests are simultaneously represented and preferences constantly evolving and negotiated, the real puzzle is why there is any semblance of continuous common policy development at all. However, the competences of the European Union are undeniably expanding. Such achievement in the area of the EU's external policies is all the more striking because common foreign and security policies as well as internal policies with external dimensions such as energy, the environment and migration have seen significant expansion since the ratification of the Maastricht Treaty in 1993. The concept of 'normative power Europe' provided a fresh perspective on the international role of the European Union that pushed beyond the classic 'civilian power' conceptualization and related debates, and asserted instead that the EU was in essence a post-national political community and 'a promoter of norms which displace the state as the centre of concern' (Manners 2002: 236). In terms of its validity as a policy framework, what is most significant is that for Manners the EU's identity and ontological foundations are central to analyzing its foreign policy, as well as its 'actorness' and capabilities. The starting point is confronting the nature of the actor and taking this into consideration in the very framing of the questions posed by researchers. According to Manners, the EU's identity as a normative power derives from three sources: (1) historical context – i.e., the legacy of two world wars; (2) hybrid polity – i.e., a Union as a post-Westphalian order with supranational and international institutions; (3) political-legal constitutionalism – i.e., élite-driven, treaty-based nature of European integration.[5]

Confronting whether the EU as a normative power is a 'contradiction in terms', Manners and others have shown that NPE is rather a conceptualization that can in fact accommodate multiple conceptions of power both civilian and military. Manners's intention was not to displace or argue against those characterizations but to add to them and to underscore the crucial component of the EU's fundamental, ideational nature. In sum:

> The idea of pooling sovereignty, the importance of a transnational European Parliament, the requirements of democratic conditionality, and the pursuit of human rights ... are constitutive norms of a polity which is different to existing states and international relations. Thus the different existence, the different norms, and the different policies which the EU pursues are really part of redefining what *can* be normal in international relations.' (Manners 2002: 253).

Moving from concept towards a theoretical approach, Manners and Whitman (2003) developed more extensively the notion of the EU's international identity by elucidating what they refer to as the 'reflexive dimension' and illustrating how the distinctiveness of the polity and the role representations of the EU should be thought of as a 'difference engine', meaning the addition of international elements to the already complex and multifaceted identities extant among Europeans. What is of significance here is the very notion that reflexivity plays an important part of the construction and representation of the EU's international identity and presumably its actions. In almost every international action undertaken or any attempt at a common foreign policy position, the EU seemingly undergoes an exercise in what Holland (2002) describes as an identification and legitimation internal process coupled with an external process of justification and projection. Soft power, civilian power, ethical power or even military power conceptions, and analysts who enlist such conceptions to explicate EU foreign policy developments or specific EU external actions, often miss this critical, cognitive dimension that is inherent in NPE as a theoretical construct. It is necessary, however, to anchor this ideational interpretation with empirical referents.

The extent to which the EU has been able to project power and influence and diffuse its norms is one test by which scholars are able to demonstrate the conceptual and theoretical advantages of the normative power Europe concept *vis-à-vis* other approaches to understanding the EU's international 'actorness'. However, accepting the normative basis of the EU does not mean that the EU always acts in a normative way, nor that the norms it seeks to promote are necessarily or always consistent with its own, very unique internal principles. This is precisely why NPE is more than a concept; it is a theoretical grounding that guides analytical work attempting to make sense of and explain the role of the EU as a global actor. As Birchfield has argued elsewhere, one should be cautious in distinguishing between the theoretical and empirical functions of NPE and 'avoid conflating NPE as an analytical construct with NPE as an uncontested interpretation of what the EU says and does' (Birchfield 2011: 144).

Manners admonishes scholars attempting to analyze EU policy and influence empirically without posing the questions of why the EU is or is not acting or 'how we might judge what the EU should be doing in world politics' (Manners 2008: 45). In contrast, the normative power approach seeks to contribute to a better understanding of the principles promoted by the EU – those recognized within the United Nations (UN) system as universally applicable – how it acts, and its impact. He argues that 'we must judge the EU's creative efforts to promote a more just, cosmopolitical world in terms of its principles, actions and impact', which, he suggests, translate into the maxims of 'living by example', 'being reasonable' and 'doing least harm' (Manners 2008: 47). These three normative anchors also constitute the empirical core of NPE and the tripartite analytical framework that illustrates its capacity to interpret and explain the EU policy-making process. First, one must 'examine the constitutive principles of the EU and how these become promoted as aims and objectives of the EU in world politics' (Manners 2008: 55); second, the tripartite analysis must 'look at how the EU promotes its constitutive principles as actions and policies in world politics' (Manners 2008: 57); and the third, part of the tripartite analysis is 'to consider the impact and outcomes of EU actions taken to promote its constitutive principles in world politics' (Manners 2008: 58). This epistemological clarification serves to unify the normative, theoretical foundations and the empirical imperatives of the NPE approach and reveals that policy – from formation to implementation to evaluation – can be of central concern and in fact must be if we are to advance NPE as a research program. Next, we shall consider whether these overarching features of the NPE approach meet the common assessment criteria delineated for traditional policy frameworks.

ASSESSMENT CRITERIA FOR POLICY FRAMEWORKS: HOW DOES NPE HOLD UP?

In one of the most widely used primers for evaluating theories of the policy process, Paul Sabatier specifies four overarching criteria by which to assess the key strengths and limitations of contending frameworks. First, each framework must 'do a reasonably good job of meeting the criteria of a scientific theory' (Sabatier 2007: 8), meaning that its concepts and propositions be clear and internally consistent, allowing for specification of hypotheses that can be tested and falsified. Second, each framework must engender a good deal of conceptual development and empirical testing. Third, a framework should be a positive theory that aims to explain the policy process. Importantly, for our consideration of normative power Europe, the author adds that 'it may also contain some explicitly normative elements' (Sabatier 2007:8). The fourth criterion is that each framework must address the conventional set of factors that analysts examining the policy process typically look at, such as conflicting values and interests, information and institutional arrangements. The seven frameworks evaluated in Sabatier's important and widely referenced volume were selected for analysis and comparison based on whether or not they met such criteria. Therefore, subjecting the NPE framework to this same set of criteria facilitates an objective and reasonably stringent method of judging its validity as a policy framework.

With regard to the first and second criteria, the NPE framework clearly specifies the concepts of pooled sovereignty, transnationalism, requirements of democratic conditionality and the pursuit of human rights as constitutive norms of a different kind of polity. Such concepts are not necessarily original to the NPE framework, but they are internally consistent and interlinked in ways other theories in the EU studies literature are not, and they can easily be conceived as variables to be operationalized, employed theoretically and tested empirically as causal drivers of behavior. As we shall see, in the survey of NPE scholarship there is indeed development in the literature illustrating both continued conceptual refinement as well as empirical testing. The third criterion demands that frameworks represent a positive theory whose goal is to explain the policy process, though Sabatier mentions normative elements are allowed. Here it is important to revisit the three specifications Manners laid out in his original argument. To paraphrase, NPE can be characterized ontologically as it depicts the EU as a changer of norms, and secondly it has a positivist dimension as the EU *acts* to change norms and finally, the framework has a normative element promoting the idea that the EU *should* act to spread its norms throughout the international system. Manners stated forcefully that NPE seeks to understand both the causal and constitutive elements of the EU's principles and actions, as well as their impact. This language affirms that NPE can be enlisted in the social scientific enterprise and this positivist dimension invites us to hypothesize, measure and test these various concepts and ideas in the real world. Most importantly, NPE seeks to determine whether the EU is an agent of change via norm promotion in the international system. This is not a theoretical question but one that compels analysts to examine the formation and evaluation of real policies.

The final criterion suggests that policy frameworks examine factors that those studying the policy process conventionally explore, such as values, interests, information flows and the role of institutions. Like constructivism, NPE is more concerned with values and ideas than are conventional policy frameworks but institutions are also an important object of analysis especially the transnational EU parliament. Coincidentally, it is interesting to point out that Sabatier did not include constructivism as one of the frameworks in his first volume published in 1999, but was persuaded to add it in the second edition of 2007.

Likewise, NPE may not spring to mind as an example of a policy framework, but as the foregoing enumeration of assessment criteria illustrates, NPE is indisputably concerned with the classic questions that most policy researchers address. NPE can guide those who are interested in why certain items get onto the agenda in the first place, as the pursuit of ending capital punishment powerfully illustrates. For those more interested in the formulation and implementation stages of the policy process, NPE would tend to accentuate the transnational institutional element as opposed to resorting to the traditional intergovernmental versus supranational modes of explanation. Evaluation is also a central concern of policy analysis, and the focus of most NPE empirical research is chiefly concerned with the EU's external policies and actions. In addition to evaluating whether or not a particular EU foreign policy met with success or failure, of centrality is also the emphasis on the normative character of the action. Is it what the EU should be doing in terms of its own principles and norms and its desire to infuse those norms internationally?

In the context of the EU's foreign or external policies, another key question is whether an action constitutes a policy and whether one could reasonably call it an EU policy if only a subset of EU member states chooses to take action or pursue a policy strategy in a given situation. I enlist the following observation from John Peterson for a partial response.

> One reason why assessments of European foreign policy vary so widely is because it is unclear how the EU's success as a global actor should be measured. There is no question that the Union is far more active internationally than its founders ever imagined it could be. In several policy areas, especially economic ones, it is a global power. No other international organization in history has even tried, let alone claimed, to have a 'common' foreign policy. (Peterson 2008: 218)

Two important points arise here regarding the question of parameters and the notion of power. EU external policy is complex and ranges from classic foreign policy questions, such as what is the EU policy toward Iran's nuclear development, to the use of trade sanctions to military intervention or collective peacekeeping missions. Such debates are peripheral to the main objective of this contribution, but it is sufficient here to acknowledge that there is a substantial body of wide-ranging policies that are clearly external, and though coherence and effectiveness depends, as Peterson suggests, on the degree of consensus among its members, we are not addressing those evaluative questions here. Note that Peterson clearly affirms that, in the economic realm, the EU is a 'global power', and certainly trade or commercial policy is one of the oldest and most developed external policy areas of the EU and – unlike foreign, defense and security policies – is truly a 'common' policy, as opposed to the latter that are largely negotiated in the second pillar (pre-Lisbon) or via intergovernmental mechanisms. It is the assertion of the term 'power 'that is of critical importance here, particularly how we measure the success of the EU as a global actor. A critical reckoning of the EU's power and how it wields it sets the NPE framework apart from most rationalist or realist approaches to the EU as a global actor. Both Manners and Whitman have been concerned to show that what matters more than determining what kind of power the EU is or is not is a conscious effort on the part of analysts to evaluate the motivations for, the principles and values behind, and the consequences of the exercise of power by the EU in the world. So, with regard to the measurement problem Peterson raised, within the NPE tripartite framework that element has been clearly specified.

Peterson argues that it was in fact the gap between the EU's growing economic power and the lack of a corresponding degree of political clout that encouraged the creation of the Common Foreign and Security Policy (CFSP). 'This new system overlapped with but did not replace the Community system. Over time, it incorporated a nascent European Security and Defence Policy (ESDP)' (Peterson 2008: 18). Drawing on another key author's argument, Peterson points out that: 'Confusingly, the CFSP and ESDP are mainly labels for "institutions that *make* [policies] but *are* not proper policies" in themselves' (Peterson 2008: 18, quoting Jørgensen 2006: 509; emphasis original), which brings us to another difficulty in systematic analysis of both the content of EU foreign policy and the policy-making process in this domain. However, as an overview of NPE scholarship and a comparison with other policy approaches will show, a focus on the NPE's analytical toolkit rather than its use as yet another competing theory of international relations is not only truer to Manners's original intent, it also yields better scholarship.

NORMATIVE POWER EUROPE AND CONTENDING APPROACHES OF POLICY FORMATION

Engaging with Bickerton over the dogged dilemma of legitimacy and the EU's lack of a unified political order, Manners reiterates that the EU's political construction is one where 'state, supranational and transnational politics coexist and compete' (Manners 2011: 241). In other words, unlike the conventional International Relations (IR) and theoretically oriented debates, or the Hix (1994) inspired comparative politics approaches, what is novel about the NPE framework is that it introduces a different heuristic whereby this institutional and ideational multiplicity is not assumed away, nor dismissed as theoretically implausible or methodologically or analytically intractable. Transnational policy formation needs better theorization and empirical analysis, and NPE, as an original framework for studying the EU, may be better equipped methodologically than other models that have been borrowed and modified from either comparative politics or International Relations.

Whether or not the EU functions like a state or is rather a *sui generis* political entity is a central question that continues to drive a great deal of debate, but perhaps the more contentious division is between state-centric and non-state-centric approaches to understanding European integration. The former largely rejects supranationalist or federalist perspectives or interpretations of developments in EU history, and generally draws insights from realist theories of International Relations to explain those developments as products of inter-state bargaining and compromises reached through intergovernmental nego-tiations. Moravcsik's seminal text *The Choice for Europe* (1998) is perhaps the defining work of this approach, and the central tenet articulated therein is (unsurprisingly) that European integration can be best understood 'as a series of rational choices made by national leaders' (Moravcsik 1998: 18).

In contrast, those applying non-state-centric approaches are much more willing to acknowledge the autonomy of action and power of supranational or community level institutions and élites. These approaches can be loosely seen as descendants of the neo-functionalist school, whose founding text was Haas's 1958 classic *The Uniting of Europe*, wherein the critical concept of pol-itical spillover was elaborated. Political spillover refers to the gradual conver-gence of interests and beliefs of national élites in response to the integration process. Haas asserted that:

> Political integration is the process whereby political actors in several distinct national settings are persuaded to shift their loyalties, expectations and politi-cal activities toward a new centre, whose institutions possess or demand jur-isdiction over the pre-existing national states. (Haas 1958: 16)

In no way discounting the role of member states and their élites in the inte-gration process, there is, nonetheless, recognition that the supranational insti-tutions and the leaders within them are independent actors in their own right. Thus, this phenomenon of supranationalism – Community-level actors, ideas, and interests – could be seen as the primary object of inquiry and locus of analysis of those working in the non-state-centric tradition. NPE certainly sits more com-fortably within this tradition, yet its focus when it comes to policy-making pro-cesses is as interested in the transnational element as the supranationalist one. For example, Birchfield (2011) argues that both energy policy and the growing role of the EU in development aid cannot be understood within the old frameworks that rely on either comparative policy analytic concepts or traditional IR or foreign policy lenses. Both of these policy fields require a simultaneous focus on the trans-national dimension that is most clearly exhibited by the increasingly active role of the parliament as a critical institutional player in both instances. Authors employ-ing the NPE concept and framework who have focused on the 'deliberative nature' of policy formation (Orbie 2011; Smith 2011b) as well those critical of its absence internally (Bickerton 2011; Diez 2005) underscore what Manners and Whitman (2000) spelled out in acknowledging the polycentric nature of the EU, and particularly the coexistence of supranational and transnational delib-erations alongside and amidst state-level politics.

Mirroring broader debates in International Relations and comparative poli-tics, constructivist approaches are also on the rise in EU studies.[6] Sharing with historical institutionalists the notion that ideas and identities matter, con-structivists and NPE scholars explore how integration processes are transform-ing the nature of the state system and the political, social and cultural identities therein. While important conceptual innovations, such approaches are perhaps not as powerful for understanding why and how certain policies evolve upward to the EU level and what specific roles are played by the EU institutions in creating and sustaining that legal and policy migration. This is not necessarily a flaw in the NPE or constructivist frameworks, but rather a deliberate limitation in analytical scope or ability to address that particular set of questions. Uncommon for many approaches, NPE asks both its analysts and its subjects of study (EU actors themselves) for greater reflexivity. For example, in one study conducted by Diez and Pace (2011) the authors were able to show how the universalist and normative discursive strategies actually concealed the short-term focus of its own self-interests. Because EU officials have assimilated the normative rhetoric,[7] there is a direct opening for critical reflection and policy learning. The point here is that many of the purported shortcomings of the NPE approach stem from new empirical tests of the concept in practice. One such example is Emma Stewart's analysis of EU norm promotion and its new neighborhood policy where she finds the NPE approach incapable of fully explaining EU actions in the region of the South Caucasus. In large part, this results from its lack of a clear policy towards Russia and the ways in which the politics of energy security seem to impede principled action.[8] The bottom line in this case, as in others such as Juncos's (2011) analysis of EU activities in Bosnia, are instances where EU interests and practices undeniably trump its norms. Rather than giving the realists the upper hand, this merely focuses our attention on the importance of not assuming interests the way many rationalists and realist frameworks do, but rather unearthing them through a critical comparison of the discourse with the actual behavior and impact on the ground.

Disentangling norms and interests is not an easy task, as Diez (2005) has warned, but as many of the new applications of the NPE concept show this is where real explanatory purchase lies – particularly if we can confirm instances where there is no distinction between norms and interests. This, of course, requires the internal and continual ethical political development of the EU itself. NPE approaches stand to gain from what constructivists have advanced – carefully unpacking the processes of identity and norm construction. Likewise, constructivism could benefit from the tripartite mode of analysis that NPE approaches are beginning to generate, such as the ones mentioned here but also Bicchi (2006) and Sjursen (2006), which bring sociological institutionalism and legal analysis (respectively) to bear on the question of the gaps between normative aspirations of the EU's foreign and external affairs and its real influence regionally and globally. It should be noted that this is a policy failure, not a shortcoming of the policy framework. Many criticize the normative power Europe approach when they find empirical evidence of the EU's hypocrisy or double standards or sheer lack of influence in international arenas, without recognizing that it is the holistic, ethically grounded concepts that are being tested against real world examples in the first place, whereas most other approaches are not even concerned with such questions. This is precisely the added value of infusing reflexivity explicitly into the analytical framework.

Whereas constructivism and sociological institutionalism may be competing frameworks with NPE in that they also are interested in uncovering ideational and normative factors that influence or impede policymaking, all of these approaches rely on assumptions about the kind of institutional environment in which ideas and identities are embedded. For NPE the emphasis is upon the transnational character and the hybridity of the EU's political institutions. A plethora of studies employs some form of governance approach,[9] but one of the earliest and most influential is the multi-level governance approach formulated by Marks (1992) and Hooghe and Marks (2001). Their approach emphasizes the open-ended nature of the EU system within which a diverse range of actors operates at different levels from the local to the international, where all have the potential to wield influence. Attention to multiple levels rather than a privileging of one in particular is where we can see a number of complementarities between the multi-level governance and NPE approaches.

Some theories of multi-level governance do attempt to go beyond traditional analyses, which focus on competing national and EU level interests. Rather, multi-level governance scholars insist that EU policy is shaped by cross-national and cross-institutional actors/alliances that work together towards common objectives in issue areas and reflect a 'melding' of states 'into a multi-level polity' (Hooghe and Marks 2001 27) As Warleigh has pointed out, new theories and approaches to studying the EU must 'address what appears to be a rather different world of policymaking, in which not only the range of actors involved, but also the very ways they produce policy, have changed. This shift is often thought of as one from "government" to "governance"' (Warleigh 2006: 78). However, alone the policy-based literature and related concepts seem analytically inadequate to fully explain why new policy formation, such as that of the energy field, and other external policies, such as climate change or the extension of Common Security and Defence Policy (CSDP) emerge in the first place. Having an anchoring in normative and ideational factors that the NPE framework provides may yield deeper analytical and explanatory power of the positive role of EU level institutions.

The vagueness and lack of analytical focus on non-state-oriented institutional actors like the Commission and the European Parliament render many conventional policy approaches ineffective and largely inapplicable to the analysis of EU external policy formation, where more than traditional member state interests are also playing driving roles, such as the role of the EU parliament in shaping reform of EU development policy (Birchfield 2011) or the elaboration of the EU's distinctive 'human security' approach (Martin 2011). Thus, it appears that the frameworks conventionally employed to understand EU policy-making too often offer only partial explanations and are inadequate to the deeper aim of understanding how the institutional architecture within the EU fundamentally shapes the process, especially with regard to foreign or external policies, but also the degree of transnational deliberation as opposed to strictly intergovernmental or supranational-led negotiations. Instead, many studies are now combining various polity- and policy-oriented explanatory frameworks in efforts to more fully understand EU policy-making. Notable among these are the combination of multi-level governance and policy network theory as advocated by Warleigh (2006) and Bache (2008). Per Ove Eikeland (2011) employs this synthetic approach to powerful effect in a recent analysis of the EU's third internal energy market package. As he frames it:

> The *supranationalist* perspective inspires our long-term analysis of the power of EU institutions vis-à-vis member-state governments, while a *policy network* perspective underlies our analysis of influence by non-state agents on the Commission proposal.' (Eikeland 2011: 3)

Eikeland's study accentuates the tensions and complexities involved, even when isolating the analysis to one single dimension of a particular EU policy, albeit a complex one with both internal and external dimensions: energy policy. The multi-level governance approach does not deny that the state is an important feature in decision-making (perhaps even the most important), but asserts that the EU represents a new type of polity where the state no longer monopolizes European-level policy-making or, for that matter, even the aggregation of domestic policy interests. This is completely consistent with a core assumption of the NPE framework and should also be seen as compatible with most constructivist positions. Thus, the analytical concepts and theoretical assumptions of the multi-level governance framework could also accommodate an interest in the independent role of norms and normative principles, allowing for an assessment of their operationalization and exercise within the EU institutions themselves.[10]

An implicit defense of the validity and usefulness of the NPE framework may be discerned in the following passage excerpted from a recent *JEPP* publication assessing the EU's strategic vision and capacity as a global actor:

> Evaluations of policy ideas and strategies require some appropriate basis for comparison. Comparing the EU to a state is both inappropriate and limiting considering the EU's supranational aspects. Comparing the EU to other inter- national organizations is more appropriate, but still limiting, in that the EU's institutions and ambitions go well beyond the capacities of other most other international organizations. In my view the main reference point for evaluating EU 'actorness' is Europe's own history: do we see greater co-operation, integration, and principled foreign policy action by the EU today as compared to 10, 30, or 50 years ago? The answer clearly is yes. (Smith 2011a: 18)

As this section has shown, the NPE framework posits theories that would help to empirically substantiate or refute the claims made by this author, as well as evaluate the impact of those purportedly principled policies. Furthermore, the fact that NPE scholars are assessing the EU's external policies across diverse domains from trade to neighborhood policy to peacekeeping missions suggests that NPE is indeed operating as a policy framework.

CONCLUSION

The formation of policies that have both external and internal dimensions, as most of the EU level foreign policies increasingly do (e.g., environmental and energy policies as well as immigration issues), is not well understood in the current policy or the general EU studies literature. Related research puzzles may necessitate more complex policy models that take both issue and institutional complexity into account as they address critical aspects of the policy process from the formation to the implementation and the evaluation stages. As suggested in the previous section, NPE, constructivism and multi-level governance approaches share some core assumptions and are interested in many of the same dependent and independent variables. Two distinct advantages of the NPE approach are its attention to transnational politics and a position of critical reflexivity deriving from the normative framing, both from the point of view of the orientation of the analyst and the object being studied. Some recent empirical applications of the NPE concept show that despite its beginnings as chiefly concerned with understanding the EU's international identity, the NPE framework may be enlisted in more rigorous hypothesis or theory testing exercises and evidence-based explorations of the processes by which the EU formulates it external policies, as well as systematic evaluations of the content and impact of such policies. Such studies range from the analysis of norm promotion in the areas of the EU's new neighborhood policy (Patton 2009; Stewart 2011) to the creation of new strategic narratives (the EU's new human security agenda) for reconciling normative power and readiness to use coercive force (Martin 2011) to an investigation of the EU's core labor standards and its commercial policies (Orbie 2011). Even within this short list, one can identify at least three preoccupations of the NPE research agenda that speak to this project of comparing the relative strengths and weaknesses of various approaches to the EU policy process and which may serve to better inform researchers as they seek to make felicitous choices about the merits and deficiencies of competing frameworks. First, all NPE researchers are concerned to identify the nature of power and how it is constituted within and exercised by the EU. Second, whether explaining the emergence of a policy or its impact, there is a persistent concern with the relationship between principles (normative grounding in the EU sense but intentionality more broadly) and outcome or impact. Finally, for research questions oriented towards understanding the values-based, idea-driven nature of some aspects of EU policy formation in the external realm, the NPE framework is a useful theoretical guide. Future research employing the NPE framework should fully exploit the tripartite analytical method Manners has laid out and put the toolkit to work to better explain when and why transnationalism is a salient predictor of policy formation and outcomes, and to assess the impact and the difference that has been theoretically and conceptually attributed to the EU as a normative power.

Biographical note: Vicki Birchfield is Associate Professor in the Sam Nunn School of International Affairs and Co-Director of the Center for European and Transatlantic Studies at the Georgia Institute of Technology, USA.

ACKNOWLEDGEMENTS

I wish to thank Nikolaos Zahariadis and the anonymous reviewers for their helpful comments on early drafts.

NOTES

1 http://www.tandf.co.uk/journals/access/rjpp.pdf (accessed 24 February 2012).
2 http://www.tandf.co.uk/journals/access/rjpp.pdf (accessed 24 February 2012).
3 Manners does note that one of the key challenges for studying the EU in world politics is to find methods for understanding the constructions of this hybrid political organization without reifying its particularities or confusing different for unique or *sui generis* (see Manners 2002: 240, 2011: 241).
4 http://www.tandf.co.uk/journals/access/rjpp.pdf (accessed 24 February 2012).
5 For a fuller elaboration, see Manners (2002: 240–1).
6 In fact, as early as 1999 the *European Journal of Public Policy* devoted a special issue to 'The Social Construction of Europe'. For an incisive overview of constructivism and EU studies, see Checkel (2006).
7 Bickerton (2011: 28) cites the famous interview with Commission President Barroso (quoted also by Peterson 2008) where he argued that the EU is 'one of the most important normative powers in the world'.
8 See Stewart's chapter, 'Mind the normative gap? The EU in the South Caucasus', in the Whitman (2001) volume, where she demonstrates the EU's inability to fully transmit its norms of democracy and human rights and where its incoherent policies aggravate an already complicated region.
9 Richardson (2001) provides an excellent overview of the various approaches that apply concepts of governance and suggests how such studies contribute to better understanding of the complex system of governance within the EU, including clearer analysis of the various actors (state, non-state, supranational institutions and interest groups) and their mechanisms of co-ordination.
10 Pollack's synopsis of the governance approach makes this connection quite clear. 'First, the governance approach theorizes EU governance as a non-hierarchical, mobilizing networks of private as well as public actors, who engage in deliberation and problem-solving efforts guided as much by informal as by formal institutions. Secondly, the practitioners of the governance approach are suspicious of "off-the-shelf" models, advocating the need for a new vocabulary to capture the distinctive features of EU governance. Thirdly, students of EU governance often (although not always) emphasize the capacity of the EU to foster "deliberation" and "persuasion" – a model of policy-making in which actors are open to changing their beliefs and their preferences, and in which good arguments can matter as much as, or more than, bargaining power. Fourthly, governance theorists frequently express a normative concern with the "democratic deficit" in the EU, with many emphasizing the potential for the EU as a "deliberative democracy"' (Pollack 2010: 35).

REFERENCES

Bache, I. (2008) *Europeanization and Multi-Level Governance: Cohesion Policy in the European Union and Britain*, Lanham, MD, and Oxford: Rowman and Littlefield.

Bicchi, F. (2006) 'Our size fits all: normative power Europe and the Mediterranean', *Journal of European Public Policy* (13): 286–303.

Bickerton, C. (2011) 'Legitimacy through norms: the political limits to Europe's normative power', in R. Whitman (ed.), *Normative Power Europe: Empirical and Theoretical Perspectives*, London: Palgrave Macmillan, pp. 25–44.

Birchfield, V. (2011) 'The EU's development policy: empirical evidence of "normative power Europe"?', in R. Whitman (ed.), *Normative Power Europe: Empirical and Theoretical Perspectives*, London: Palgrave Macmillan, pp. 25–44.

Checkel, J. (2006) 'Constructivism and EU Politics', in K.E. Jørgensen, M.A. Pollack and B. Rosamond (eds), *Handbook of European Union Politics*, London and Thousand Oaks, CA: Sage, pp. 507–525.

Diez, T. (2005) 'Constructing the Self and changing others: reconsidering "normative power Europe"', *Millennium: Journal of International Studies* 33: 613–36.

Diez, T. and Pace, M. (2011) 'Normative power Europe and conflict transformation', in R. Whitman (ed.), *Normative Power Europe: Empirical and Theoretical Perspectives*, London: Palgrave Macmillan, pp. 210–24.

Eikeland, P.O. (2011) 'The third internal energy market package: new power relations among member states, EU institutions and non-state actors?', *Journal of Common Market Studies* 49: 243–63.

Haas, E. (1958) *The Uniting of Europe*, Stanford, CA: Stanford University Press.

Hix, S. (1994) 'The study of the European Community: the challenge to comparative politics', *West European Politics* 17(1): 1–30.

Holland, M. (2002) *The European Union and the Third World*, New York: Palgrave.

Hooghe, L. and Marks, G. (2001) *Multi-Level Governance and European Integration*, Lanham, MD: Rowman and Littlefield.

Jørgensen, K. (2006) 'Overview: the European Union and the world', in K.E. Jørgensen, M.A. Pollack and B. Rosamond (eds), *Handbook of European Union Politics*, London and Thousand Oaks, CA: Sage, pp. 507–25.

Juncos, A. (2011) 'Power discourses and power practices: the EU's role as a normative power in Bosnia', in R. Whitman (ed.), *Normative Power Europe: Empirical and Theoretical Perspectives*, London: Palgrave Macmillan, pp. 83–102.

Manners, I. (2002) 'Normative power Europe: a contradiction in terms?' *Journal of Common Market Studies* 40: 235–58.

Manners, I. (2008) 'Normative ethics of the European Union', *International Affairs* 84: 45–60.

Manners, I. (2011) 'The European Union's normative power: critical perspectives and perspectives on the critical', in R. Whitman (ed.), *Normative Power Europe: Empirical and Theoretical Perspectives*, London: Palgrave Macmillan, pp. 226–47.

Manners, I. and Whitman, R.G. (eds) (2000) *The Foreign Policy of EU Member States*, Manchester: Manchester University Press.

Manners, I. and Whitman, R.G. (2003) 'The "difference engine": constructing and representing the international identity of the European Union', *Journal of European Public Policy* 10: 380–404.

Marks, G. (1992) 'Structural policy in the European Community', in A.M. Sbragia (ed.), *Euro-Politics: Institutions and Policy-Making in the 'New' European Community*, Washington, DC: Brookings Institution, pp. 191–224.

Martin, M. (2011) 'Human security and the search for a normative narrative', in R. Whitman (ed.), *Normative Power Europe: Empirical and Theoretical Perspectives*, London: Palgrave Macmillan, pp. 187–209.

Moravcsik, A. (1998) *The Choice for Europe: Social Purpose and State Power from Messina to Maastricht*, Ithaca, NY: Cornell University Press.

Orbie, J. (2011) 'Promoting labour standards through trade: normative power or regulatory state Europe?', in R. Whitman (ed.), *Normative Power Europe: Empirical and Theoretical Perspectives*, London: Palgrave Macmillan, pp. 161–86.

Patton, S. (2009) 'The European Union as a normative power: Europe's new neighbourhood and energy policies', Master's thesis, Georgia Institute of Technology, Atlanta, GA.

Peterson, J. (2008) 'The EU as a global actor', in E. Bomberg, J. Peterson and A. Stubb (eds), *The European Union: How Does it Work? The New European Union Series*, 2nd edn, New York: Oxford University Press.

Pollack, M. (2010) 'Theorizing EU policy-making', in H. Wallace, M. Pollack and A. Young (eds), *Policy-Making in the European Union. The New European Union Series*, 6th edn, New York: Oxford University Press.

Richardson, J. (ed.) (2001) *European Union Power and Policy Making*, 2nd edn, London: Routledge.

Sabatier, P. (ed.) (2007) *Theories of the Policy Process*, Boulder, CO: Westview Press.

Sjursen, H. (2006) 'The EU as a "normative" power: how can this be?', *Journal of European Public Policy* 13(2): 235–51.

Smith, M.E. (2011a) 'A liberal grand strategy in a realist world? Power, purpose and the EU's changing global role', *Journal of European Public Policy* 18(2): 144–63.

Smith, M. (2011b) 'The European Union, the United States and global public goods: competing models or tow sides of the same coin?' in R. Whitman (ed.), *Normative Power Europe: Empirical and Theoretical Perspectives*, London: Palgrave Macmillan, pp. 127–40.

Stewart, E. (2011) 'Mind the normative gap? The EU in the South Caucasus', in R. Whitman (ed.), *Normative Power Europe: Empirical and Theoretical Perspectives*, London: Palgrave Macmillan, pp. 65–82.

Warleigh, A. (2006) *European Union: The Basics*, London: Routledge.

Whitman, R. (ed.) (2011a) *Normative Power Europe: Empirical and Theoretical Perspectives*, London: Palgrave Macmillan.

Whitman, R. (ed.) (2011b) 'Norms, power and Europe: a new agenda for study of the EU and International Relations', *Normative Power Europe: Empirical and Theoretical Perspectives*, London: Palgrave Macmillan, pp. 1–24.

Learning in the European Union: theoretical lenses and meta-theory

Claudio M. Radaelli and Claire A. Dunlop

ABSTRACT   The European Union may well be a learning organization, yet there is still confusion about the nature of learning, its causal structure and the normative implications. In this contribution we select four perspectives that address complexity, governance, the agency–structure nexus, and how learning occurs or may be blocked by institutional features. They are transactional theory, purposeful opportunism, experimental governance and the joint decision trap. We use the four cases to investigate how history and disciplinary traditions inform theory; the core causal arguments about learning; the normative implications of the analysis; the types of learning that are theoretically predicted; the meta-theoretical aspects and the lessons for better theories of the policy process and political scientists more generally.

INTRODUCTION

In public policy analysis, learning is often defined as a process of updating beliefs about policy based on lived or witnessed experiences, analysis or social interaction (Dunlop and Radaelli 2012). Previous studies have categorized instrumental learning (i.e., how actors learn how to improve on public policy); social learning, with paradigmatic changes reflected in policies as well in the socially dominant policy ideas; and political learning, when learning affects power and influence, e.g., governments learn how to use policy to raise the probability of re-election (Gilardi 2010; May 1992; Zito and Schout 2009). However, learning as a *process* is often problematic for social scientists. Researchers have found it easier to observe the products of learning, such as exemplary policy lessons, the usage of new policy instruments and dramatic changes in the direction of public policy. Measurement is also difficult in this field: how do we know that what we observe is learning and not something else (May 1992)?

In this contribution, we look at learning as one of the promising frameworks mentioned by the guest editor in his introduction (Zahariadis 2013). But from where do we start? Since the study of the European Union (EU) is characterized by prominent theories of integration, one could rather conventionally think that the learning framework can simply be extracted from the major theories of

European integration. However, these theories are concerned with the explanation of why member states create, and maintain, the institutions of the EU, not with policy dynamics. Though we will encounter integration theories more than once in our journey through learning, we cannot predetermine the essential features of the framework by starting from theories.

Previous research and a full special issue of this journal (Zito and Schout 2009) alert us to four dimensions we should consider when theorizing EU learning. First, policy learning is intimately connected to governance. Consequently, we consider theoretical lenses on learning that shed light on the dimension of governance (Zito and Schout 2009: 1115). Second, learning combines capacities and strategies at the individual level – what is often refereed as the 'agency' dimension of public policy – with system-level characteristics. Learning revolves around capacity and strategies at the individual–organizational level (Schout 2009). But for learning to be a characteristic of public policy, we need to explore how complex organizations, and entire policy subsystems, learn, and with what effects on policy. Third, previous research has often been biased because it has neglected instances in which learning is stymied or simply does not occur (Zito and Schout 2009: 1110, Table 1). It follows that we also need theoretical lenses that explain blockages and hindrances to learning (Radaelli 2009). Fourth, different research traditions matter. Zito and Schout (2009: 1111–12) mention comparative public policy, diffusion studies and International Relations (IR). Authors differ sharply in term of their understanding of learning as outcome or process (Zito and Schout 2009: 1115), and whether they focus on reflexive social actors or 'bargainers'. This shows that there is also an ontological and epistemological dimension. In consequence, following Jupille (2005), we need to consider theory and meta-theory jointly.

This leads us to select perspectives that meet the four criteria; i.e., they situate learning in the context of governance, link individual agency to structure, cover the full spectrum of variation (including zero learning), and vary by ontological-epistemological foundations. In addition, we want our cases to provide explicit theoretical foundations and seem *prima facie* equipped to cope with the complexity described in the introduction (Zahariadis 2013). To maximize variability, we select the perspectives from different time periods (to control for the effects of a given socio-political context on the development of theory; see Wiener and Diez [2004: 13]; Rosamond [2000: 10]) and disciplinary traditions.

These criteria do not predetermine sample size – provided that the cases generate variation in each individual criterion, the inclusion of additional cases does not necessarily increase explanatory leverage. Thus, we selected a sample of four cases. They are the political community of Deutsch and his collaborators (Deutsch *et al.* 1957); Cram's purposeful opportunism (Cram 1993); experimental governance (Sabel and Zeitlin 2008); and the joint decision trap associated to the work of Fritz Scharpf (Scharpf 1988). Of course, this sample is a drop in the ocean of articles on learning in the EU. We neglect the work of Ernst Haas (1958) (but we have Deutsch to represent connections with Haas) and the literature on experts and expertise in EU public policy (but see

Montpetit [2009]). Further, Cram's (1993) paper is distinctively slighter and more idiosyncratic than the others.[1] Thus, ours is not a review of the field but rather an attempt to find cases that have the characteristics described by Zahariadis (this collection), and meet our criteria and vary on the dimensions of interest here. To generate theoretical leverage, we raise the following research questions:

1. How do history and disciplinary concerns inform the emergence of the four cases?
2. What are the core causal arguments?
3. What are the normative implications of the analysis?
4. What do the cases tell us about learning as 'dependent variable'?
5. What is the role of meta-theory?
6. What are the lessons for the wider community of public policy analysts and political scientists, whether they engage with the EU or not?

We take these questions in order. We expose the core causal arguments, the normative implications (including arguments about the design of EU institutions), the dependent variable, the meta-theoretical features and the lessons for political scientists. Finally, we conclude on the pros and cons of our method and relate the contributions to the theories of European integration, and beyond.

HISTORY AND THE DEVELOPMENT OF SOCIAL SCIENCES

Deutsch's analytical lenses developed in a unique historical context. (Deutsch *et al.* 1957)[2] For Deutsch, a Sudetan German born in Czechoslovakia who was adamantly opposed to Nazism and for this reason had to leave his country, the major historical question was how to build and sustain communities that could leave in peace. The spectre of World War II and the presence of the Cold War shaped the way in which his generation thought about the *explanandum*, with the theme of peace dominating their scientific inquiry.

Instead, the joint decision trap (JDT) emerged from reflections about the institutional hindrances to change affecting federal systems. Scharpf found the core features of his model in German federalism. The JDT of the EU, essentially, is a projection of some critical reflections on the suboptimal performance of German federal *Politikverflechtung*. The original piece (Scharpf 1988; the original in German dates back to 1983) appeared during the period of slow pace in integration characterized by Caporaso and Keeler with the label 'the doldrums years' (Caporaso and Keeler 1995; see also their qualifications). In this context, Scharpf's JDT provided a powerful explanation of why it was so difficult to reap the benefits of integration. Even when the pace of integration accelerated again, with the Single European Act (and later Economic and Monetary Union and enlargement), the JDT remained a cornerstone of explanations of decision-making. During the years, the development of veto players theory by George Tsebelis (1995) has provided yet another angle to observe the JDT mechanisms, thus embedding Scharpf's model into broader political science models (Scharpf 2011). Scharpf's actor-centred institutionalism is yet another more general framework to account for the JDT (Scharpf 2011: 221).

Yet again different, but always with effects on the *explanandum*, is the context faced by Cram (1993) one decade later. In the 1990s the Commission looked increasingly capable of entrepreneurship and expansion of policy tasks. As a bureaucracy, the Commission became the natural object of attention of public policy scholars, well-equipped to analyse bureaucratic politics. Asymmetric policy developments also presented an opportunity for theoretical advances, exploited chiefly by Majone (1996). Redistributive and tax policies were not growing, whilst regulatory policy was on the rise – a structural feature of EU policy that is still present now. These developments were theoretically intriguing in terms of timing, too. Some policies remained dormant and effectively non-existent for long periods of time, after which they grew rapidly, even before the treaties acknowledged them. These historical and intellectual conditions provided a window of opportunity for the take-off of the theoretical analysis of EU public policy, which, thanks to Majone's work, was redirecting its attention to the EU as 'regulatory state' (Caporaso 1996).

Let us yet again move the clock one decade forward. Whilst Cram in the 1990s was concerned with the capacity of the Commission to foster task expansion and exercise entrepreneurship (Cram 1993), Sabel and Zeitlin wrote in 2008 that 'the EU is today in crisis, and will likely remain so for several years to come' (Sabel and Zeitlin 2008: 272). However, underneath this prolonged state of crisis, these authors saw 'the institutional equivalent of a Cambrian explosion of life forms' (Sabel and Zeitlin 2008: 278); that is, a formidable process of innovation affecting the whole governance framework of the EU. They called this framework 'experimentalist governance' or directly deliberative polyarchy. The essence of the framework is to 'learn from difference'.

This interest in innovative modes of governance is a product of the EU history of the time; but as in the other cases, we can also trace back this research focus by considering the evolution within specific fields of the social sciences. For reasons of limited space in this contribution, we can only refer to Sabel's reflections on learning – leaving aside Zeitlin's own intellectual progress. An important strand in his research is the balance between learning and monitoring (Sabel 1994). On the one hand, complex organizations need to monitor the behaviour of their units. On the other, monitorability may destroy the conditions for learning. The latter requires innovation, the possibility to make mistakes, and explorations that, if monitored and disciplined in their early stages, may not blossom into learning but retreat into perfunctory compliance or conformism. Thus, for Sabel, organizational and social behaviour is very much a matter of tackling the trade-off between learning and monitoring.

Sabel, however, went further and showed how the trade-off between monitoring and learning can be overcome. Information gathered in networks (Piore and Sabel 1984) and generated by monitoring (Sabel 2006) can be used to improve performance, and ultimately to feed back into learning processes. Drawing on both organizational theory and socio-legal studies, Sabel was interested in explaining how learning is produced under strategic uncertainty, when the solution to the problem is not known in advance. In these conditions, governance structures must work like radars that collect and distribute information and problem-solving, because solutions cannot be found at the centre. This is reminiscent of Deutsch's (1966) observation about communication networks that see ahead ('lead'), implement their decisions quickly ('lag'), and deal with elements competing for attention in the system ('load'). Sabel then generalized these intuitions about monitoring and learning to governance, and, in two co-authored articles (Cohen and Sabel 1997; Gerstenberg and Sabel 2002), added democracy to the equation. He argued that in deliberative polyarchies the experience of a multiplicity of actors provides a repertoire of responses to current problems. It is this concrete experience that thus generates innovation and change – not the classic representative that responds in an assembly governed by majority rule on the basis of abstract problems of which she has no direct experience. Directly deliberative forms are therefore based on learning from experience and deliberation. The network radar observed at the level of firms (Sabel 2006) has eventually mutated into democratic governance.

THE CORE CAUSAL ARGUMENTS

To illustrate the diagnostic modes of analysis, we focus on the core causal arguments in our four cases. For Deutsch, two strands of his work of interest here, concerning integration theory and learning respectively, have attracted slightly different communities of scholars. His major contribution to the problems of peace is his 1957 co-authored book on *Political Community and the North-Atlantic Area*. Yet, it is in his 1963 work *The Nerves of Government* that we find a model of learning. If the former is often cited by scholars of the EU in the context of integration theories (although the book was not concerned with the European Community),[3] it is the latter that was celebrated among policy theorists (Heclo 1972).

For our purposes, however, it is useful to keep the two strands together. In *Political Community and the North Atlantic Area*, the analysis of 10 historical processes leads Deutsch and his collaborators to identify the conditions for the creation of security communities – i.e., a group of people who have become integrated, sharing an expectation that the resolution of social problems requires peaceful means and institutions. Some of these conditions revolve around identity – the sense of community that binds people together and stabilizes expectations about behaviour. These habits – Deutsch clarifies – at any point in time are taken for granted, but, historically, values and expectations have to be acquired by processes of social learning. The second set of conditions concern Deutsch's transactional theory; that is, the multiplicity and balance of transactions – communications, mobility of individuals and trade on one side, and their institutional counterparts on the other, contribute to integration in a major way.

The third set of conditions refers to the capabilities of the core institutions. These capabilities are necessary to manage what Deutsch called 'the burden', or the 'traffic load of messages and signals upon the attention-giving and decision-making capabilities of the persons or organizations in control' (Deutsch *et al.* 1957: 41). In turn, capabilities are the characteristics of a learning system. It is here that his cybernetic approach to politics plays a very important role. In *The Nerves of Government*, political organizations are described in terms of their learning capacity (Deutsch 1966: ch. 10). Organizations are held together by communication. To transmit information, to react to signals, to exercise self-controlling mechanisms and manage feedback are the key functions of political systems – in this image, a political system is a type of cybernetic system, in line with the broader systemic turn in political science exemplified by David Easton (1965). This way, learning becomes the core *explanans* via the notion of capabilities.

If Deutsch provides a celebration of learning, Scharpf (1988) moves into the darker zone where learning is not possible. He does that by dint of a straightforward application of Coasian thinking about transaction costs. Sub-optimal decision-making outcomes are caused by the direct representation of member states into the EU key decisions. Direct representation is the first condition for the JDT. Unanimity, *de facto* or *de jure*, makes it impossible to override the concentrated interests of individual units that object to the decision – this is the second condition. The third condition is that the EU works under the classic Community method where participation of the member states is compulsory. When we consider the three conditions together, we are under a unique mode of decision-making, the JDT.

When decisions are taken in the JDT, they become difficult to change. Over time, a situation emerges in which the EU faces high costs of action, but the member states can no longer have the capacity to produce policy change in domains that are Europeanized. The JDT is a 'trap' only if member states cannot pursue autonomous action – owing to the legal framework of integration and the characteristics of the Community method (Scharpf 2011: 222). Consequently, the JDT is a compulsory negotiation system. Although the JDT was never meant to be a general impossibility theorem, and therefore individual EU policies may progress, the model predicts both suboptimal *policy* decisions and *institutional* stalemate, or, better:

> all possibilities of institutional transformation are entirely determined by the self-interests of national governments. And even among those who vigorously support activist and expansionary European policies are likely to hedge their bets when it comes to relinquishing their veto powers. (Scharpf 1988: 268)

To put it differently, institutional veto positions are more important than substantive policy preferences.

Over the years the JDT has inspired predictions about negative and positive integration, and product versus process regulations. Scharpf expected the JDT to be more 'virulent' in positive integration (Scharpf 2011: 225). It is difficult (under JDT conditions) to produce policies that govern markets (as opposed to policies that create markets). Product regulation can be used as a barrier against import. Although member states disagree on how to harmonize regulations, in classic battle-of-the-sexes fashion they all agree on the necessity to harmonize them. By contrast, process regulation and direct tax co-ordination face tough JDT hurdles, given the diversity of national economic and institutional structures in the EU.

How does learning play a role in the JDT? We find learning only as violation or relaxation of the conditions of the basic model. At the theoretical level, if we add to the member states the Commission as yet another strategic player (as Cram [1993] would do, see below), we find that the JDT tight conditions can be relaxed. The Commission – Scharpf (2011) acknowledged – uses its monopoly of legislative initiative and the threat of infringement procedures to alter the outcome of joint-decision negotiations. Depending on the preferences of the Commission, the overall policy trajectory towards deregulation and negative integration can be partially reversed. This leads us to the Commission as purposeful entrepreneur (Cram 1993; Schmidt 2000) – our third case.

Cram proceeds from the observation that redistributive social policy has remained practically non-existent, whilst EU social policy of a regulatory nature has expanded, with patterns and timing that cannot be explained by the presence or absence of Treaty provisions. To address asymmetric growth of EU social policy and the timing issue, Cram draws on two major contributions to theoretical policy analysis; that is, Majone's (1996) approach to the regulatory state and Guy Peters on bureaucratic politics (Peters 1992). The argument goes as follows: constrained by a limited budget, the Commission learns how to switch from grandiose projects about EU-wide redistribution to regulatory policy. The production of regulation is virtually costless to the regulator. Its major impact is on firms and citizens. The Commission cannot expand its budget freely, but gradually learns how to expand the domain of regulation.

The learning process is time-bound. The Commission – Cram argues – started with a head-on approach to social policy that only led to a perceived threat to the sovereignty of the member states. Hence major attempts to social policy harmonization were curtailed by the Council (Cram 1993: 143). Unable to intervene directly, the Commission learned how to intervene gradually, incrementally and marginally, 'without alienating national governments' (Cram 1993: 143). But learning also affects the choice of policy instruments, because the Commission, behaving as 'purposeful opportunist', over time has turned to regulation (rather than expenditure) as its major policy instrument.

Purposeful opportunism is the core causal mechanism of learning. The purposeful opportunist works outside the radar of the member states by building expertise and knowledge reservoirs that can be used at the earliest possible opportunity. This policy entrepreneur creates procedures and 'process policy' that can be later used as infrastructure for major policy changes. Process policy, in short,'"may be important in setting up a system conducive to further regulation' (Cram 1993: 144). Soft law plays the same function: it is essentially a way to build prerequisites for hard law without raising the concerns of the member states. The conclusion is that the Commission expands its power: 'making use of the bureaucratic skills, building upon EC declarations, instituting social programmes, setting up observatories and carrying out research projects, the Commission is continually preparing for the next opportunity to create new policies' (Cram 1993: 144). What is distinctive about this approach to learning, then? This causal argument explains both inertia and policy change. For long periods of time nothing seems to happen. But, when nothing seems visible on the major radar of integration theory, the Commission orchestrates a layer of procedures, soft law, technical expertise that can be deployed if and when the opportunity arises.

This theme of innovation becomes even more prominent in experimentalist governance. Here the core causal propositions are extended from the analysis of monitoring and learning, adding the governance dimension of polyarchy. Essentially, the direct deliberative polyarchy framework is calibrated onto the EU. The latter is polyarchic because of its 'multipolar ... distribution of power, in which no single actor has the capacity to impose her own preferred solution without taking into account the views of the others (Sabel and Zeitlin 2008: 280). This is one of the two possible conditions for experimentalist governance. As mentioned, the other is strategic uncertainty. This type of uncertainty makes it impossible to calculate pay-offs of alternative courses of action, or, as they put it:

> policy makers recognise that they cannot rely on their strategic dispositions (e.g., more market vs. more plan) to guide action in a particular domain (or equivalently that they do not know *how* to achieve their declared goals). (Sabel and Zeitlin 2008: 280; emphasis in the original).

Experimentalist governance – the causal argument goes on – emerges from three different routes: the networks of regulators in telecommunications and energy; the networked agencies dealing with drugs and occupational health and safety; and the so-called open method of co-ordination at work in several domains of EU public policy. This new architecture does not emanate from the treaties. It is functional rather than institutional – or structural. The key functions, in fact, can be performed by different institutional arrangements. It is informal but subject to permanent institutional revision and waves of proceduralization that give the false impression of 'informality'.

The essence of experimentalist governance is to connect different actors in multi-level networks that monitor, diffuse information on policy performance and generate feedback. Instruments like annual reporting and peer review create the necessary informational conditions for monitorability. Socialization in multi-level networks creates opportunities for exchanging and adapting local solutions found in one place to another place. Thus, 'deliberative polyarchy is a machine for learning from diversity, thereby transforming an obstacle to closer integration into an asset for achieving it' (Sabel and Zeitlin 2008: 276).

DESIGN AND NORMATIVE IMPLICATIONS

These causal arguments have also prescriptive implications. First, they suggest how a learning system should be designed. Second, they can be used to develop normative appraisals.

Let us start with design issues. Deutsch explains that:

> the ability of any political decision system to invent and carry out fundamentally new policies to meet new conditions is clearly related to its ability to combine items of information into new patterns, so as to find new solutions that may be improbable in terms of their likelihood of being discovered, but relevant once they are discovered and applied. (Deutsch 1966: 163)[4]

Learning itself is nothing but a special capacity. Deutsch talks of the learning capacity of systems, based on the presence of resources that are 'available for unexpected recommitment' (Deutsch 1966: 164), that is, resources that can be redeployed by the system when the environment signals new challenges or opportunities. How to design a political system (for the EU) like this and whether the EU we know is this type of learning system are two important questions.

For Deutsch, the EU should be designed with in-built feedback, which goes beyond the capacity to respond to the environment – a design principle that exposes today's limitations of designing co-ordination in the eurozone exclusively as responses to the financial markets. Action must be produced in response to information. But the information input 'includes the results of its own action in the new information by which it modifies its subsequent behaviour' (Deutsch 1966: 88). Learning capacity is more advanced than the classic ('mechanistic' for Deutsch [1966: 185]) concept of equilibrium. In fact, a learning system is in principle equipped to pursue changing goals. Deutsch (1966: 187) comments that feedback is suitable for catching up with a trajectory like the one of a zigzagging rabbit. The EU we know today is not a learning system of this type.

Turning to normative appraisal, learning does not have to be necessarily 'benevolent'. On the one hand, learning can become deutero-learning: the organization 'learns to learn' (Deutsch 1966: 169, citing Gregory Bateson's concept). On the other, Deutsch acknowledges the possibility of self-destructing learning, which means that the organization 'learned something that has reduced its subsequent capacity to learn, or its subsequent capacity to control its own behaviour' (Deutsch 1966: 169).

A JDT designer would instead pay attention to institutional changes that can alter the three conditions that – according to Scharpf (1988) – hinder learning and policy change. But others have criticized the JDT for not having considered changes that take place even under unchanging institutional settings. Outside the radar of veto players, experts groups use subterfuge to get around the JDT (Heritier 1997). Socialization in bureaucratic settings creates preconditions for learning and ways to reduce veto players considerations in what has been labelled an emergent European executive order (Trondal 2010). A deep crisis or a major threat is often a condition for switching from bargaining to problem-solving attitudes – in which case the JDT dissolves (Falkner 2011: 4). The European Court of Justice, critics of the JDT have observed, has produced exits from the JDT. However, the European Court of Justice does not control their judicial agenda and, unlike the Commission, cannot set a trajectory (e.g., towards positive integration [Scharpf 2011]). Interestingly, the normative appraisal remains negative, whether we accept the original JDT or are open to the critiques. Courts do not necessarily improve on the legitimacy of the EU. Subterfuge may be even worse than the original JDT, where at least the responsibility for the lack of change is clear.

Equally negative are the normative implications of purposeful opportunism, which has similarities with 'integration by stealth' (Majone 2005). In a recent article, interestingly based on her interview data and material that date back to the early 1990s, Cram takes the position that the normative justification for the opportunistic behaviour of the Commission is poor. Generalizing from social policy to 'new modes of governance', Cram argues that these modes:

> are no less 'stealthy' and no more democratic than the traditional attempts of the Commission to expand its competence and capacity to govern. Indeed, new modes of governance, now increasingly widespread, may act as a fig-leaf for undemocratic practices. (Cram 2011: 649)

By contrast, some policy instruments of experimentalist governance open up pathways to a more accountable EU. To illustrate, peer review and procedural requirements to report policy performance in public expose national public administrations to contestation in an information-rich environment, and promote a form of political competition rooted in the quality of arguments rather interests. This leads to a relatively optimistic normative assessment. Sabel and Zeitlin deny vigorously that theirs is a technocratic model. Quite the opposite; the accountability properties of EU experimentalist processes have democratizing effects on domestic politics, and, via feedback, enhanced domestic accountability may reverberate on the EU itself (Sabel and Zeitlin 2008: 277). The design implications are clear: we should spend less time in thinking about institutional reforms at the treaty level and support with adequate resources the networks that provide monitoring and learning.

THE DEPENDENT VARIABLE: LEARNING TYPES AND PROCESSES

We are now ready to consider the question about the type of learning found in our four cases. Recall that May (1992) differentiates between instrumental, social and political learning. Scharpf (1988) identifies areas where instrumental learning is technically possible and desirable, but institutional settings hinder it. In different ways, Sabel and Zeitlin (2008) and Deutsch (1966) engage with social learning. Their perspective is broad, beyond the individual policy subsystem, arguably because in the end they are concerned with the dimension of governance.

Additionally, Sabel and Zeitlin put more emphasis on policy subsystems where they account for instrumental learning. By contrast, Cram (1993) is clearly interested in how bureaucratic actors learn how to pursue their strategies. The Commission does not have electoral objectives (so this is not exactly the classic form of political learning [Gilardi 2010]). But Cram's type is still political because it is aimed at increasing integration at the expense of policy coherence and democratic accountability. Learning is not instrumental in the sense of improving on public policy. It is a process functional to strategy. Turning to Scharpf (1988), he is concerned with explaining lack of learning, so he falls in the residual category of 'blocked learning' rather than 'social', 'political' or 'instrumental'.

Having looked at learning as outcome, what about the process? Deutsch (1966) conceptualizes political systems as networks of communication channels where information from both inside and outside that system, past and present, steers society. Learning processes are indeed evolutionary – emerging through feedback processes, where political systems respond and adjust to the flow of information. In Scharpf's (1988) analysis, when learning does occur, it is in spite of the joint decision trap. It is the result of autonomy that actors have won for themselves against the structural odds (Dunlop and Radaelli 2012). Briefly, for Scharpf there is learning in the shadow of hierarchy, i.e., within a rule-bound, institutionally rich environment where agency is still possible (in line with his actor-centred premises). The purposeful opportunist story is one of strategic learning – the Commission wants to expand its power without increasing its costs. For Sabel and Zeitlin (2008), the key to innovation is a deliberative process – and consequently learning through reflexivity.

META-THEORY

In exploring the meta-theoretical and methodological assumptions, we are clearing the underbrush (Bevir 2008) from this literature. We take inspiration from Jupille's (2005) analysis of the EU studies literature, adapting some his dimensions to the nature of this article. To begin with, we already found that the *explanandum* in the four cases has emerged within certain historical conditions and *different disciplinary traditions*. These 'provide different sets of received wisdoms' (Jupille 2005: 211). Our four ways of theorizing learning arise from different disciplines: International Relations (Deutsch *et al.* 1957); theoretical policy analysis (Cram 1993); socio-legal studies and organizational theory (Sabel and Zeitlin 2008); and political science/comparative politics (Scharpf 1988).

Our second cut at meta-theory concerns Jupille's social theoretic category (Jupille 2005: 211). Wendt (1999) puts Deutsch squarely in the camp of the precursors of constructivism. Adler (2002: 99) reminds us that 'Deutsch himself was not a constructivist – constructivism had yet to make its way from sociology to political science – and favoured a positivist epistemology', although he had 'an indelible influence on later development in constructivism'. Sabel and Zeitlin (2008) fit the Deweyan tradition of pragmatism, which rejects the absolute assumptions of rational choice and constructivism in terms of logic of action. For pragmatists, there is an ongoing redefinition of ends and means generated by reflective actors engaged in practical experience.[5] Scharpf's JDT is inspired by rational choice institutionalism. Sub-optimal decisions are the default outcomes in complex federal systems where self-interested behaviour by actors – member states in this case – unanimity and compulsory partici-pation combine to create decisions that are difficult to reform or revisit. Argu-ably for purposeful opportunism, the correct label is strategic constructivism (Jabko 2006): the Commission pursues a certain set of goals, albeit it cannot calculate the future, it can only gamble on the future. Under these conditions, the Commission orchestrates a strategy of integration (i.e., reliance on regu-lation, preparation of repositories of expertise when time is not ripe for action, and purposeful opportunism) that is socially constructed.

The next dimension – *ontology* – is whether social phenomena exist indepen-dent of our conceptualization of them or are constructions which result from actors acting on their beliefs. The contrast is between 'objective' reality and social or 'subjective' ontology. An objective ontology is found only in Scharpf (1988), where the barrier to learning – the JDT – is an objective institutional reality that exists independent of political actors' knowledge of it. The work of Deutsch, Cram and Sabel/Zeitlin is all underscored by subjective ontology (Deutsch *et al.* 1957; see also Deutsch 1966; Cram 1993; Sabel and Zeitlin 2008). Here actors are socially constituted by their interaction within, and experi-ence of, their context. As for *epistemology*, following Searle (1995), we distinguish between a social and an objective epistemology. In contemporary objective epis-temology, social scientists are aware of the value-laden nature of observation and that social actors respond to different types of stimuli introduced by researchers in the social environment. Yet, they think that with research design techniques one can reduce bias and make valid inferences drawn from empirical observations. This is because in an objective epistemological tradition there is still some dis-tance between observer and the social phenomena that are observed. A value jud-gement like 'Mountain A is prettier than Mountain B' is, following Searle (1995), epistemically subjective. But 'Mountain A is higher than Moutain B' is objective – and so are many statements in the social sciences, like '[T]his year total amount of money borrowed by the government is higher than last year'. For Scharpf an objective epistemology is aligned with an objective ontology. The other authors start from a different, social ontology, but their empirical work does not clash with an objective epistemology. As demonstrated by Searle (1995), it is possible to combine an objective epistemology with a social ontology – note Adler's (2002: 99) remark that Deutsch was a precursor of constructivist ontology but anchored to positivist epistemology.

We have already mentioned the role of *structure and agency*. Let us make a few more remarks on this dimension. Both Deutsch *et al.* (1957) and Scharpf (1988) underline the importance of structures in enabling and constraining learning opportunities. For Deutsch, the political system is a network of communication channels whose default position is to enable feedback from which learning flowed. Failure to learn is a failure of government to steer information flows and relate knowledge and forecasts back to decision-making. Scharpf, too, has a structuralist approach. No learning is the default position of decision-making complex federal systems. Where learning does occur, it will be as the result of an opportunity or a hitherto unknown structural hole which agents carve out or exploit. This theme of the ability of agents to create political opportunities that structures do not appear to allow is emphasized by Cram. Sabel and Zeitlin similarly give the agent a prominent role in analysis. Learning is the result of actors exchanging information in a dense network governed by certain rules.

Complexity has both an institutional and an issue dimension. Zahariadis (2013) rightly observes that theoretical lenses do not have the same explanatory power in addressing the two dimensions. In terms of our four major contributions, the JDT moves from institutional complexity, but it also has leverage at the issue level, considering the causal arguments about the differential development of negative and positive integration. At the opposite, Deutsch and his collaborators (1957) were majorly concerned with institutional analysis rather than individual policy issues. In between the extremes we found purposeful opportunism, a lens or approach that tackles issue complexity directly, and institutional complexity indirectly, and experimentalism. Sabel and Zeitlin (2008) do not separate out the institutional and the policy level. They rather provide causal arguments about the rise of a mode of governance where institutions and issue complexity interact, and then they explain why certain issues are more suitable for experimentalism than others.

LESSONS DRAWN

Since theories of integration are not there to explain learning but to make sense of integration, we started somewhat unconventionally from four approaches grounded in cybernetics, theoretical policy analysis, network-based reflexivity and deliberation, and rational choice institutionalism.

Eclectic researchers could use the core causal propositions for different purposes. Transactional theory and the JDT are particularly useful for research projects aiming at the polity level. For example, a project on how the EU has responded, in terms of governance structures, to financial instability should consider the causal role of capabilities on the type of learning produced by the EU. A JDT perspective would add the analysis of the institutional blockages that explain decisions and non-decisions of the EU leaders. Instead, experimentalism and purposeful opportunism direct researchers towards core causal mechanisms that take place at the policy level – although in the long term they have polity implications. Major governance innovations do not necessarily take place at the level of treaties and formal constitutional politics. Policy sectors incubate change that is not immediately visible because it is subject to permanent institutional revision. Procedures create reservoirs of knowledge that can be exploited by purposeful opportunism. Today, perhaps purposeful opportunism is less a characteristic of the Commission: it points us towards the behaviour of the European Central Bank instead. Purposeful opportunism is also a bridge towards the multiple stream model (Kingdon 1984). However, purposeful opportunism can also be integrated in historical institutionalism, given the emphasis on time, and more precisely on the long-term effects of day-by-day, incremental and seemingly irrelevant procedures (Pierson 1996).

One could also turn purposeful opportunism on its head, and argue that if the Commission learns, why shouldn't the member states take note of what is going on and react? This invites an analysis of the information asymmetries and other post-delegation problems well-known to scholars of regulation (Pollack 1997). Another option is to turn the JDT on its head and explore exits (Falkner 2011). But subterfuges, the intervention of the courts, the use of threat by the Commission, and other exits are not normatively desirable. They may reduce legitimacy and aggravate the democratic deficit of the EU. This may generate instrumental and political learning, but fail in terms of social learning.

To explore social learning, we need to turn to Deutsch (1966) and experimentalism. For policy theorists, Deutsch has the great merit of having moved our understanding of social learning from equilibrium to adaptation to changing goals. For him, a learning system effectively responds to changing goals, rather than simply creating the conditions for equilibrium among its constitutive units. This is a perceptive comment during this critical phase of EU integration, given that the EU policy change is very much a journey, perhaps, to paraphrase Deutsch, a 'zigzagging journey', rather than a destination.

Reflecting on the current state of the EU at a major crossroad, a deep crisis can offer exits from the JDT. But Deutsch shows the possibility of dysfunctional learning. In terms of better theories, the presence of a crisis invites us to reflect on the relationship between learning processes and change. Although we normally assume that actors first learn (process of preference modification) and then change (outcome), behavioural and experimental economics claim that actors can reshape their preferences owing to situational and cognitive constraints. When the very existence of integration and domestic state structures is questioned by an extremely challenging context (a sort of 'change or die' situation), decision-makers may choose whatever non-incremental change enables them to survive, even if their core preferences would tell them to go for more limited change. They might well learn *ex-post*, as a consequence of change. If this is true, we may not need entrepreneurship and visionary leaders to get out of a crisis.

Experimentalism offers the conditions for non-incremental change to emerge and also find its own way of delivering on accountability and social legitimacy. The model of experimental governance, however, does not envisage social learning as major discontinuity taken via some sort of history-making decision. It is definitively more evolutionary – historical decisions may then congeal the progress made in evolutionary ways.

CONCLUSIONS

To conclude, we answer the question about the theoretical leverage of these theories beyond EU studies. One limitation of the four cases is that taken together they look like a patchwork: neither are they alternative and mutually exclusive, nor do they complement nicely. However, there is a connection between experimentalism and cybernetic theories.[6] Experimentalist architectures produce exactly the feedback from implementation to learning capacity which Deutsch (1966) saw as a core feature of well-performing systems, but was unable to pin down in institutional-organizational terms. In a sense, experimentalism goes back to Deutsch's original problem formulation with new theoretical tools. In turn, these tools are drawn on EU policy innovations that did not exist when Deutsch was developing his cybernetic approach.

Another limitation is the lack of specific tools for measuring learning: although there are causal arguments about the presence or absence of learning, there is much less on key empirical tests, measurement, scales, and so on. While we cannot integrate the four approaches in one single testable theory of learning valid across political systems, the four approaches are extremely well-suited to travel well outside the EU in terms of suggesting core causal arguments and standards of normative appraisal. Deutsch elaborated his conjectures in a fully comparative framework (Deutsch *et al.* 1957; Deutsch 1966). Features of purposeful opportunism exist in various bureaucratic systems, not just in the European Commission. Democratic-deliberative governance is a property of policy systems that appeared in the United States before they entered the EU. And, the JDT is a model of blocked decision-making that is not restricted to the EU. But this is exactly the nature of these theories: they travel well because they were not generated with an EU imagery or EU vocabulary in mind. Their authors did not think they had to explain a special case but rather solve more general political science, decision-making and governance puzzles. In this connection, these learning theories contribute to making the field of EU studies less *ad hoc* and more embedded with mainstream social science.

Future research could use our findings to explore EU learning by connecting theory and meta-theory – thus contributing to a richer understanding of this phenomenon. We have also barely mentioned how to turn learning theories into design issues – a topical question, given the current crisis of the eurozone. Another lesson for future research is to focus on constraints and limitations of learning, as well as on cases where learning occurs, because this can provide a lot of information of how institutions structure, facilitate or hinder learning. Finally, learning is not a monolith (Dunlop and Radaelli 2012). When researchers move from concepts to measurement, it is important to qualify our dependent variable as social-evolutionary, political-strategic, reflexive-experimentalist learning, or learning as escape route from traps and shadow of hierarchy.

Biographical notes: Claudio M. Radaelli is professor of political science at the University of Exeter, where he directs the Jean Monnet Centre of Excellence on European Governance. Claire A. Dunlop is senior lecturer in politics, University of Exeter.

ACKNOWLEDGEMENTS

This contribution is based on research carried out with the support of the European Research Council grant on Analysis of Learning in Regulatory Governance, ALREG (http://centres.exeter.ac.uk/ceg/research/ALREG/index.php). The authors wish to express their gratitude to Jan Pieter Beetz, Oliver Fritsch, Sophie Heine, Gjovalin Macaj, Kalypso Nicolaïdis, the other authors in this collection – and in particular its editor, Nikos Zahariadis – and two anonymous referees.

NOTES

1 We are grateful to a reviewer for this observation.
2 The reference to lenses is appropriate, considering that Deutsch studied optics in England for two years.
3 Interestingly, although Sandholtz and Stone-Sweet (1998) celebrated Deutsch for his intuitions about the causal effects of transactions, social exchange and communication on integration, they cite his work on security communities but not *The Nerves of Government* (Deutsch 1966) . The work by Sandholtz and Stone-Sweet was in any case instrumental in rediscovering the importance of Deutsch for integration theorists.
4 Citations are from the first paperback edition of 1966 but the original hardback dates to 1963.
5 We wish to thank a reviewer for this insight.
6 We owe this remark to a reviewer.

REFERENCES

Adler, E. (2002) 'Constructivism and international relations', in W. Carlsnaes, T. Risse and B., A. Simmons (eds), *Handbook of International Relations*, London: Sage, pp. 95–118.
Bevir, M. (2008) 'Meta-methodology: clearing the underbrush', in J.M. Box-Steffensmeier, H.E. Brady and D. Collier (eds), *The Oxford Handbook of Political Methodology*, Oxford: Oxford University Press, pp. 48–70.
Caporaso, J. (1996) 'The European Union and forms of state: Westphalian, regulatory or post-modern?' *Journal of Common Market Studies* 34(1): 29–52.
Caporaso, J. and Keeler, J. (1995) 'The European Union and regional integration theory', in C. Rhodes and S. Mazey (eds), *The State of the European Union, Volume 3: Building a European Polity?* London: Longman, pp. 29–62.
Cohen, J. and Sabel, C.F. (1997) 'Directly-deliberative polyarchy', *European Law Journal* 3(4): 313–42.
Cram, L. (1993) 'Calling the tune without paying the piper? Social policy regulation: the role of the Commission in European Community social policy', *Policy and Politics* 21(1): 135–46.
Cram, L. (2011) 'The importance of the temporal dimension: new modes of governance as a tool of government', *Journal of European Public Policy* 18(5): 636–53.
Deutsch, K.W. (1966) *The Nerves of Government*, New York: The Free Press.
Deutsch, K.W. *et al.* (1957) *Political Community in the North Atlantic Area: International Organization in the Light of Historical Experience*, New York: Green-

wood Press.

Dunlop, C.A. and Radaelli, C.M. (2012) 'Systematizing policy learning: from monolith to dimensions', *Political Studies*, doi: 10.1111/j.1467-9248.2012.00982.x.

Easton, D. (1965) *A Systems Analysis of Political Life*, New York: John Wiley & Sons.

Falkner, G. (ed.) (2011) *The EU's Decision Traps. Comparing Policies*, Oxford: Oxford University Press.

Gerstenberg, O. and Sabel, C.F. (2002) 'Directly-deliberative polyarchy: an institutional ideal for Europe?' in C. Joerges and R. Dehousse (eds), *Good Governance in Europe's Integrated Markets*, Oxford: Oxford University Press, pp. 289–341.

Gilardi, F. (2010) 'Who learns from what in policy diffusion processes?' *American Journal of Political Science* 54(3): 650–66.

Haas, E. (1958) *The Uniting of Europe*, Stanford, CA: Stanford University Press.

Heclo, H. (1972) 'Review article: policy analysis', *British Journal of Political Science* 2: 83–108.

Heritier, A. (1997) 'Policy-making by subterfuge: interest accommodation, innovation and substitute democratic legitimation in Europe -perspectives from distinctive policy areas', *Journal of European Public Policy* 4(2): 171–89.

Jabko, N. (2006) *Playing the Market: A Political Strategy for Uniting Europe, 1985–2005*, Ithaca, NY, and London: Cornell University Press.

Jupille, J. (2005) 'Knowing Europe: metatheory and methodology in EU studies', in M. Cini and A. Bourne (eds), *Palgrave Advances in European Union Studies*, Basingstoke: Palgrave, pp. 209–32.

Kingdon, J.W. (1984) *Agendas, Alternatives and Public Policy*, Glenview, Illinois: Harper Collins.

Majone, G.D. (1996) *Regulating Europe*, London: Routledge.

Majone, G.D. (2005) *Dilemmas of European Integration. The Ambiguities and Pitfalls of Integration by Stealth*, Oxford: Oxford University Press.

May, P.J. (1992) 'Policy learning and failure', *Journal of Public Policy* 12(4): 331–54.

Montpetit, E. (2009) 'Governance and policy learning in the European Union: a comparison with North America', *Journal of European Public Policy* 16(8): 1185–203.

Peters, G.B. (1992) 'Bureaucratic politics and the institutions of the European Community', in A. Sbragia (ed.), *Europolitics. Institutions and 'Policy-Making' in the 'New' European Community*, Washington, DC: Brookings, pp. 75–122.

Pierson, P. (1996) 'The path to European integration. A historical institutional analysis', *Comparative Political Studies* 29(2): 123–63.

Piore, M.J. and Sabel, C.F. (1984) *The Second Industrial Divide: Possibilities for Prosperity*, New York: Basic Books.

Pollack, M. (1997) 'Delegation, agency, and agenda setting in the European Community', *International Organization* 51(1): 99–134.

Radaelli, C.M. (2009) 'Measuring policy learning: regulatory impact assessment in Europe', *Journal of European Public Policy* 16(8): 1145–64.

Rosamond, B. (2000) *Theories of European Integration*, Basingstoke: Palgrave.

Sabel, C. (1994) 'Learning by monitoring: the institutions of economic development', in N. Smelser and R. Swedberg (eds), *Handbook of Economic Sociology*, Princeton, NJ: Princeton University Press, pp. 137–65.

Sabel, C.F. (2006) 'A real time revolution in routines', in C. Hecksher and P., S. Adler (eds), *The Firm as a Collaborative Community: Reconstructing Trust in the Knowledge Economy*, Oxford: Oxford University Press, pp. 106–56.

Sabel, C.F. and Zeitlin, J. (2008) 'Learning from difference: the new architecture of experimentalist governance in the EU', *European Law Journal* 14(3): 271–327.

Sandholtz, W. and Stone Sweet A. (eds) (1998) *European Integration and Supranational Governance*, Oxford: Oxford University Press.

Scharpf, F.W. (1988) 'The joint-decision trap: lessons from German federalism', *Public Administration* 66(6): 239–78.

Scharpf, F.W. (2011) 'The JDT model. context and extensions', in G. Falkner (ed.), *The EU's Decision Traps. Comparing Policies*, Oxford: Oxford University Press, pp. 217–36.

Schmidt, S.K. (2000) 'Only and agenda setter? The European Commission's power over the Council of Ministers', *European Union Politics* 1(1): 37–61.

Schout, A. (2009) 'Organizational learning in the EU's multi-level governance system', *Journal of European Public Policy* 16(1): 1124–44.

Searle, J. (1995) *The Construction of Social Reality*, New York: Free Press.

Trondal, J. (2010) *An Emergent European Executive Order*, Oxford: Oxford University Press.

Tsebelis, G. (1995) 'Decision-making in political systems: veto players in presidentialism, parliamentarism, multicameralism and multipartyism', *British Journal of Political Science* 25: 289–325.

Wendt, A. (1999) *Social Theory of International Relations*, Cambridge: Cambridge University Press.

Wiener, A. and Diez, T. (eds) (2004) *European Integration Theory*, Oxford: Oxford University Press.

Zahariadis, N. (2013) 'Building better theoretical frameworks of the EU's policy process', *Journal of European Public Policy* 20(6), doi: 10.1080/13501763.2013.781815.

Zito, A.R. and Schout, A. (2009) 'Learning theory reconsidered: EU integration theories and learning', *Journal of European Public Policy* 16(8): 1103–23.

Index

Note:
Page numbers in **bold** type refer to figures
Page numbers in *italic* type refer to tables
Page numbers followed by 'n' refer to notes